# What Do Great Teachers Say?

Do you remember a time when you used the right words at the right moment, and they made all the difference? With the aim of helping you repeat that experience every day, this book provides hundreds of examples of what we call Great Teacher Language, a technique designed to help all teachers use words to transform student behavior and parent relationships. In their years of working at the K-12 levels, educators Hal Holloman and Peggy H. Yates have identified the exact phrases and key words you can use in your classroom to address inappropriate outbursts, a lack of respect and cooperation, student conflict, and more. Great Teacher Language will enable you to transform student behavior, parent relationships, and your classroom culture.

The book features 11 Great Teacher Language Word Categories, which you'll learn how to use in terms of self-talk, student talk, and parent talk: Words of Accountability, Words of Encouragement, Words of Grace, Words of Guidance, Words of High Expectations, Words of Hope, Words of Love, Words of Relationships, Words of Respect, Words of Understanding, and Words of Unity.

Filled with helpful charts and Great Teacher Language examples, this resource will be one you turn to again and again and will make a transformational difference for your middle and high school students, their parents, and you!

**Hal Holloman** has experience as a teacher, coach, assistant principal, and principal at various levels. Currently, he is a Professor of Educational Leadership at East Carolina University and Director of the ECU Pirate Leadership Academy, where he teaches in the Masters of School Administration program and coaches new school leaders.

**Peggy H. Yates** has over 35 years of experience in the field of education, including positions as an elementary and middle school teacher, district-level K-8 curriculum and instruction director, higher education administrator, and Associate Professor in the College of Education at East Carolina University.

# *Also Available from Routledge Eye On Education*

(www.routledge.com/k-12)

**What Do Great Teachers Say? Language All Teachers Can Use to Transform Student Behavior, Parent Relationships, and Classroom Culture K-5**
Hal Holloman and Peggy H. Yates

**Classroom Management from the Ground Up**
Todd Whitaker, Katherine Whitaker, Madeline Whitaker Good

**Your First Year, 2e: How to Survive and Thrive as a New Teacher**
Todd Whitaker, Katherine Whitaker, Madeline Whitaker Good

**The Student Motivation Handbook: 50 Ways to Boost an Intrinsic Desire to Learn**
Larry Ferlazzo

**75 Quick and Easy Solutions to Common Classroom Disruptions**
Bryan Harris and Cassandra Harris

**What Do Great Teachers Say? Language All Teachers Can Use to Transform Student Behavior, Parent Relationships, and Classroom Culture 6-12**
Hal Holloman and Peggy H. Yates

# What Do Great Teachers Say?

## Language All Teachers Can Use to Transform Student Behavior, Parent Relationships, and Classroom Culture 6-12

Hal Holloman and Peggy H. Yates

Routledge
Taylor & Francis Group
NEW YORK AND LONDON

First published 2024
by Routledge
605 Third Avenue, New York, NY 10158

and by Routledge
4 Park Square, Milton Park, Abingdon, Oxon, OX14 4RN

*Routledge is an imprint of the Taylor & Francis Group, an informa business*

© 2024 Hal Holloman and Peggy H. Yates

The right of Hal Holloman and Peggy H. Yates to be identified as authors of this work has been asserted in accordance with sections 77 and 78 of the Copyright, Designs and Patents Act 1988.

All rights reserved. No part of this book may be reprinted or reproduced or utilised in any form or by any electronic, mechanical, or other means, now known or hereafter invented, including photocopying and recording, or in any information storage or retrieval system, without permission in writing from the publishers.

Portions of this book were previously published as *What Do You Say When?… Best Practice Language for Improving Student Behavior*, Routledge, 2010.

*Trademark notice*: Product or corporate names may be trademarks or registered trademarks, and are used only for identification and explanation without intent to infringe.

ISBN: 978-1-032-50882-5 (hbk)
ISBN: 978-1-032-50586-2 (pbk)
ISBN: 978-1-003-40013-4 (ebk)

DOI: 10.4324/9781003400134

Typeset in Palatino
by SPi Technologies India Pvt Ltd (Straive)

# Dedication

To our Heavenly Father—your love, grace, hope, and guidance are amazing!

To my beautiful wife, Blair—you are my soulmate and best friend. I love you!

—Hal

I dedicate this book to:

All Teachers Everywhere
You touch students' hearts and minds every day. You make a difference in our world!

My Husband
You support me and love me unconditionally. You are my best friend!

My Children
You made us a family. You are my joy and happiness!

My Grandchildren
You make my heart smile and call me Nana. You are my grand love!

My Heavenly Father
My Rock and My Salvation

—Peggy

# Contents

*List of Tables* .................................................... xii
*Meet the Authors* ................................................ xiii

   Introduction ........................................... 1

1 **Great Teacher Language: The Right Words at the Right Time** ........................................... 4

2 **The 11 Great Teacher Language Word Categories and Frameworks for Transforming Middle School and High School Student Behavior and Parent Relationships** ........................................... 8

3 **What Do Great Teachers Say on the First Day of School and the Days that Follow?** ..................... 39
   **Standard 3.1:** Setting High Expectations for All .................. 41
   **Standard 3.2:** Establishing Rules and Behavior Expectations for Success ................................. 45
   **Standard 3.3:** Creating a Culture of Community and Teamwork ......................................... 48
   **Standard 3.4:** Encouraging Life-Long Self-Management ... 51
   **Standard 3.5:** Leading by Example .......................................... 54
   **Standard 3.6:** Building Relationships with Students and Their Families ......................................... 58

4 **What Do Great Teachers Say When a Student Seems Apathetic, Passively Disengaged, or Disconnected from School?** ........................................... 69
   **Scenario 4.1:** A Student is Chronically Absent from School ............................................. 73
   **Scenario 4.2:** A Student is Consistently Tardy to School or to a Particular Class ....................... 77

Scenario 4.3: A Student is Skipping School All Day or Skipping a Particular Class During the Day ............................................................ 80
Scenario 4.4: A Student is Sleeping During Class ............... 85
Scenario 4.5: A Student is Not Working on His Assignment and Looks Confused, Stressed, Or Frustrated....................................... 89
Scenario 4.6: A Student Is Not Paying Attention to the Lesson, Is Uninterested, or Seems to Be Daydreaming In Class........................................ 91
Scenario 4.7: A Student Never Verbally Participates In Class ................................................................... 93
Scenario 4.8: A Passively Disengaged Student Has Failing Grades In Your Class............................ 96

## 5 What Do Great Teachers Say to Encourage Proper Use of Technology and Devices in the Classroom? ......... 102

Scenario 5.1: A Student is Off-task and Texting on His/Her Phone................................................. 104
Scenario 5.2: A Student is Off-task, Playing a Video Game, Watching a Video, or Watching a Movie on His Phone/Computer ................... 108
Scenario 5.3: A Student is Off-task and Listening to Music on His/Her Phone (Using Ear Buds) ................................................................ 110
Scenario 5.4: A Student is Off-task and Searching Online for Personal Reasons ......................... 113
Scenario 5.5: A Student is Plagiarizing Other People's Work and/Or Copying Answers from Online Sources ...................... 115

## 6 What Do Great Teachers Say When a Student is an Attention Seeker? ................................................... 121

Scenario 6.1: A Student is Intentionally Asking Questions to Distract the Teacher Away From the Lesson...................................... 124

Scenario 6.2: A Student Is Up Out of His/Her Seat, Looking at Another Student's Phone, Laughing, and Socializing with Other Students ............................................................ 126
Scenario 6.3: A Student is Annoying Another Student and Wanting Their Attention Either Verbally, in Writing, Or by Texting ............... 130
Scenario 6.4: A Student is Being the Class Entertainer and/or Social Influencer ............................... 132
Scenario 6.5: A Student is Verbally Monopolizing the Lesson by Answering Every Question or Constantly Asking Questions ................... 136
Scenario 6.6: A Student is Constantly Talking with Other Students During the Lesson .............. 138

## 7 What Do Great Teachers Say When a Student Outburst Happens? ........................................................ 145
Scenario 7.1: A Student Yells Out, "This Is So Boring!" ..... 147
Scenario 7.2: A Student Yells Out, "I'm Lost! I Don't Understand!" .................................................. 149
Scenario 7.3: A Student Yells Out, "Why Do We Have to Do This…? When Are We Ever Going to Need This or Use This?" ................ 151
Scenario 7.4: A Student Yells Out Profanity, "@#$%!" ....... 154
Scenario 7.5: A Student Yells Out a Verbally Aggressive Outburst and/or Acts Out a Physically Aggressive Outburst ....................................... 158

## 8 What Do Great Teachers Say When a Student Does Not Show Respect for Themselves or Others? .......... 166
Scenario 8.1: A Student is Calling Other Students Disrespectful Names and/or Making Fun of Other Students .................................... 169
Scenario 8.2: A Student is Making Inappropriate Gestures Toward Other Students and/or the Teacher ........................................... 174

Scenario 8.3: A Student is Verbally Disrespectful to the Teacher .................................................. 178
Scenario 8.4: A Student is Interrupting Another Student and/or the Teacher .......................... 182
Scenario 8.5: A Student is Taking Things That Do Not Belong to Him/Her ......................................... 185
Scenario 8.6: A Student is Demonstrating a Lack of Self-Respect .................................................. 189

## 9 What Do Great Teachers Say When a Student Refuses to Cooperate or Challenges Them? .................... 195

Scenario 9.1: A Student Consistently Asks Questions that Challenge You and/or the Lesson You Are Teaching .............................................. 201
Scenario 9.2: A Student Disagrees With You and Says, "You're Wrong! That's Not What We Were Taught Before!" ........................................ 204
Scenario 9.3: A Student Refuses to Cooperate with You and Says, "You're Not My Mom! You Can't Tell Me What To Do! You Can't Make Me Do This Work!" ................... 207
Scenario 9.4: A Student is Outwardly Angry and Blatantly Disrespectful Toward You ............. 212

## 10 What Do Great Teachers Say When a Student Conflict Occurs? ................................................. 220

Scenario 10.1: Two Students Are in a Small Disagreement and Are Not Getting Along With One Another ............................. 226
Scenario 10.2: Two Students Are Arguing with One Another .................................................................. 228
Scenario 10.3: A Student Pushes and/or Shoves Another Student ..................................................... 232
Scenario 10.4: A Student Hits Another Student ................. 234
Scenario 10.5: A Student is Bullying Another Student ..... 240
Scenario 10.6: A Student is Cyberbullying Another Student .................................................................. 246

**Scenario 10.7:** Two Students Are Physically Fighting ...... 252
**Scenario 10.8:** A Student Hits the Teacher .......................... 257

## 11 Transforming Your Middle School and High School Classroom Culture into a Great Classroom Culture to Promote High School Readiness, College and/or Career Readiness, and Life Skills ...... 265

*Index of GTL Student Behavior Scenarios* .................. 276

# Tables

| | | |
|---|---|---|
| 2.1 | The Great Teacher Language Framework for Transforming Student Behavior in the Classroom and Beyond | 26 |
| 2.2 | Great Teacher Language Framework for Transforming Student Behavior and Preparing **Middle School Students** for High School and Life | 29 |
| 2.3 | Great Teacher Language Framework for Transforming Student Behavior and Preparing **High School Students** for College and/or Career and Life | 32 |
| 2.4 | The Great Teacher Language Framework for Transforming Parent Relationships | 35 |
| 11.1 | The Great Classroom Culture Framework for High School Readiness, College and/or Career Readiness, and Life Skills | 266 |

# Meet the Authors

**Hal Holloman** has experience in elementary, middle, and high schools as a teacher, coach, assistant principal, and principal. He grew up in rural eastern North Carolina in Aulander and graduated from Bertie High School. He earned his BA in English from Wake Forest University, his Master of Arts in Educational Administration from East Carolina University, and his PhD in Educational Administration from the University of South Carolina.

Currently, he is a Professor of Educational Leadership at East Carolina University and Director of the ECU Pirate Leadership Academy, where he teaches in the Masters of School Administration program and coaches new school leaders in eastern North Carolina. His current research focuses on uncovering great educator language to coach and promote vitality and prevent burnout for school leaders, teachers, students, and parents. Dr. Holloman is co-author of the book, *What Do Great Teachers Say? Language All Teachers Can Use to Transform Student Behavior, Parent Relationships, and Classroom Culture (K-5)* and *What Do You Say When…? Best Practice Language for Improving Student Behavior*. His work has also been published in journals such as the *International Journal of Leadership Preparation*, *Journal of Positive Behavior Interventions*, *International Journal of Leadership in Education*, *School Leadership Review*, and the *Journal of Cases in Educational Leadership*. He lives in Greenville, North Carolina with his wife, Blair, and they have four children, Luke, Zeke, Jessie, and Maggie.

**Peggy H. Yates** has over 35 years of experience in the field of education, including positions as an elementary and middle school teacher, district-level K-8 curriculum and instruction director, higher education administrator, and Associate Professor in the College of Education at East Carolina University. While at ECU, she taught elementary education methods courses in classroom management and curriculum. She earned a BA in Elementary Education from Fairmont State College, a Master of Education from Tarleton State University, and a PhD in Organizational Leadership in Education from Regent University.

Dr. Yates is co-author of *What Do Great Teachers Say? Language All Teachers Can Use to Transform Student Behavior, Parent Relationships, and Classroom Culture (K-5)* and *What Do You Say When…? Best Practice Language for Improving Student Behavior*. She has also written journal articles highlighting effective teaching strategies, classroom management, and Best Practice Language. She is now retired and lives in North Carolina with her husband, Merle. She has two children, Stephanie and Adam; and nine grandchildren, Hailey, Cole, Lorelei, Maddie, Annabelle, Emmyrose, David, Brandon, and Austin.

# Introduction

This book is about great language that all middle school and high school teachers can use every day to make a difference with students and parents. We call this great language-Great Teacher Language (GTL)! From our personal teaching experiences, when student behavior disruptions occurred or when parents were disconnected from school, we would ask ourselves, "What could I say right now to make a difference with this student or this parent?" Throughout this book, you'll find hundreds of GTL examples that all middle school and high school teachers can use to make a difference "in the moment," to prepare middle school students for high school and life, and to prepare high school students for college and/or career and life. Ultimately, these GTL examples are for you to use to transform student behavior, parent relationships, and your classroom culture.

The book is divided into 11 chapters. Chapters 1 and 2 define and describe GTL and four GTL Frameworks: the GTL Framework for Transforming Student Behavior; the GTL Framework for Transforming Student Behavior and Preparing Middle School Students for High School and Life; the GTL Framework for Transforming Student Behavior and Preparing High School Students for College and/or Career and Life; and the GTL Framework for Transforming Parent Relationships. Each framework consists of the 11 GTL Word Categories – Words of Accountability, Words of Encouragement, Words of Grace, Words of Guidance, Words of High Expectations, Words of Hope, Words of Love, Words of Relationships, Words of Respect, Words of Understanding, and Words of Unity – and provides teachers with a reflective model for turning their Language of Practice into GTL.

Chapter 3 strategically focuses on GTL you can use on the first day of school with students and parents. Chapters 4 through

10 present challenging classroom behavior scenarios. Each chapter begins with the question 'What Do Great Teachers Say?' and identifies four to eight specific student behavior scenarios that are common in today's middle school and high school classrooms. In each chapter, you'll also find relevant and helpful background information related to each classroom behavior scenario. All of these chapters offer teacher-friendly charts with *GTL Reminders to Self, GTL to Share with Students, GTL to Use When Talking and Communicating with Parents,* and *GTL Classroom Activities.*

> *GTL Reminders to Self* can be used by teachers to pause and reflect on what is happening with students and parents and why it might be happening. These GTL Reminders to Self are great self-coaching reminders to consider before speaking to students and parents.
>
> *GTL to Share with Students* provides teachers GTL to use before, during or after student behavior scenarios occur. These GTL examples can be shared with an individual student, a group of students, or the whole class. Teachers can turn to the exact page in the book to find the GTL examples to use "in the moment".
>
> *GTL to Use When Talking and Communicating with Parents* provides teachers with a GTL template for phone conversations, emails, or other types of messages to help transform parent relationships.
>
> *GTL Classroom Activities* provide teachers with classroom activities that bring GTL to life as students Role-Play GTL scenarios and participate in Hit the Pause Button Discussions about Student Behavior Expectations and participate in Getting Ready for Life Discussions.

At the end of the book, we have also included an *Index of GTL Student Behavior Scenarios* that lists the 42 student behavior scenarios in Chapters 4 through 10.

In Chapter 11, we describe the Great Classroom Culture (GCC), which is built on the 11 GTL Word Categories. We present the GCC Framework for High School Readiness, College and/or Career Readiness, and Life Skills, which describes the transformational outcomes that middle school students, high school students, and their parents can experience when a teacher promotes the 11 GTL Word Categories in their classroom. We provide descriptions of the 11 GTL Word Categories and how they help middle school students be prepared for high school and life and how they help high school students be prepared for college and/or career and life. We also share how a GCC can break the burnout-to-dropout cycle; prevent student, parent, and teacher burnout; and promote vitality for you and your school community!

This book is a guide for transforming student behavior, parent relationships, and your classroom culture. Our greatest hope is that this book will become yours and become one of the favorite books in your personal library. We hope it will become frayed, raggedy, taped together in places, and full of yellow highlights and Post-it notes as you use it every day.

# 1

# Great Teacher Language

## *The Right Words at the Right Time*

Wow, did you hear that? Did you hear what that teacher said? Those words were absolutely great! What professional and inspirational teacher language! She used the right words at the right time. That student was about to (fill in the blank), and those right words at the right time made all the difference. Her Great Teacher Language (GTL) resonated with the student and served as a compass, providing clear and respectful guidance. The student listened to what the teacher said, and the student's behavior was impacted in a positive way.

We believe GTL is great language that all teachers can use every day to make a difference with students and parents. As you read this book, you will find hundreds of GTL examples you can use every day to transform student behavior, parent relationships, and your classroom culture.

### Words Matter and Great Words Really Matter

Our language is a word quilt that is made up of all the words that have been offered to us and shared with us throughout our lives. We have adopted language from teachers, parents, coaches, friends, colleagues, and others. Adopting and acquiring language from others is a significant part of who we are. How we choose to use those words will make a difference! *Words matter.*

The words we use do make a difference. They set expectations. They inspire. They resonate. They move others. They are spoken. They are written. They are heard. They are felt. They help us to understand each other. *Words matter!*

Our daily work as teachers is demonstrated by a combination of what we do and the words we say—our Language of Practice (LoP). What we say to students, what we say to parents, and what we say to ourselves constitute our LoP. Our LoP is a foundational and vital part of our teaching practice and can be honed and refined much like other skills of a trade. We, as teachers, believe that a renewed and intentional interest in the words we speak to students and parents will lead to transformational outcomes. *Our words matter!*

When teachers use great words in the form of GTL, those words will help students and parents feel cared for and understood. GTL blends accountability with respect and love. Teachers can set high expectations, offer grace and guidance, build relationships, and promote unity when they speak great words to students and their parents. GTL encourages and offers hope to students and parents all along the way. GTL can transform student behavior, parent relationships, and your classroom culture. *Great Words really matter!*

## Defining Great Teacher Language

GTL is a (1) **teacher's LoP** that (2) **resonates with others**, (3) **influences others**, and (4) **produces transformational outcomes**.

### Great Teacher Language is a Teacher's Language of Practice

On any given day in any classroom across the world, teachers are using a combination of different words that make up their LoP. For teachers, our LoP has major implications on our daily instructional practice. Earlier, we mentioned that our LoP is a foundational and vital part of our professional practice and can be honed and refined much like other skills of a trade. When our daily LoP integrates and reflects GTL, it can transform student behavior, parent relationships, and your classroom culture.

### Great Teacher Language Resonates with Others

GTL resonates with the heart. Sometimes, despite our best attempts to communicate and emotionally connect with students, our LoP can be ignored, seem irrelevant, and go in one ear and out the other without ever touching the heart. In this situation, our words make no emotional connection, have no effect on these students, and leave them feeling disconnected and unphased. GTL can create a meaningful and emotional connection with students. We believe that GTL has a resonating affective quality that can resonate with a student's heart. As GTL resonates with students' hearts, these previously unphased and disconnected students discover that they can do things they never thought they could do. GTL can transform your classroom culture as it touches students' and parents' hearts and resonates throughout your classroom and beyond as middle school students and high school students prepare for life.

### Great Teacher Language Influences Others

GTL positively influences the hearts and minds of students and parents. GTL influences and carefully guides students from being disrespectful, passively disengaged, and emotionally disconnected to becoming respectful, actively engaged, and emotionally connected. The influential quality of GTL motivates and leads students to make better choices for themselves. The job you have as a teacher has positioned you in front of a select group of young people and their parents, and they are both influenced by you! They observe you and listen to you, and you have a significant opportunity to teach them, lead them, influence their lives, and develop relationships with them in a positive way. We believe that when GTL is used consistently by teachers, it can positively influence and transform student behavior, parent relationships, and your classroom culture.

### Great Teacher Language Produces Transformational Outcomes

GTL produces transformational outcomes in student behavior, parent relationships, and classroom culture. These transformational outcomes can serve as a catalyst for creating a Great Classroom Culture (GCC) of Accountability, Encouragement, Grace, Guidance, High Expectations, Hope, Love, Relationships, Respect, Understanding, and Unity. In a GCC, all your students and their parents can expect to experience love, grace, encouragement, guidance, and high expectations for everyone's success. The more GTL is used with students and parents, the more people hear it and are transformed by it. This cycle of transformation feeds on itself and generates excitement, enthusiasm, vitality, and a confidence that success is possible for everyone! Middle school students feel confident and ready for high school and life, and high school students feel confident and ready for college and/or career and life.

In this chapter, we outlined the definition of GTL and highlighted how GTL can transform student behavior, parent relationships, and your classroom culture. We strongly believe that as we all work to find the "right words at the right time," GTL will lead to significant and transformational outcomes for you, your students, and their parents.

Chapter 2 will introduce four GTL Frameworks: one for transforming student behavior in the classroom and beyond, one for transforming student behavior and preparing middle school students for high school and life, one for transforming student behavior and preparing high school students for college and/or career and life, and one for transforming parent relationships. Each GTL Framework is composed of the 11 GTL Word Categories that make up GTL. Chapter 2 will also provide definitions of the 11 GTL Word Categories and specific GTL examples to use with students and parents.

# 2

# The 11 Great Teacher Language Word Categories and Frameworks for Transforming Middle School and High School Student Behavior and Parent Relationships

This chapter describes the 11 Great Teacher Language (GTL) Word Categories that all middle school and high school teachers can use to make a difference "in the moment," to prepare middle school students for high school and life, and to prepare high school students for college and/or career and life. These 11 GTL Word Categories are Words of Accountability, Words of Encouragement, Words of Grace, Words of Guidance, Words of High Expectations, Words of Hope, Words of Love, Words of Relationships, Words of Respect, Words of Understanding, and Words of Unity. In this chapter, we've provided specific definitions of the 11 GTL Word Categories for both students and parents. Under each GTL Word Category, you'll find two GTL examples that are specific for students and parents. We've included the ultimate behavior goal for middle school students and high school students and the ultimate partnership goal for parent relationships for each GTL Word Category. Additionally, in Chapters 3–10, you'll find hundreds of GTL examples you can use with students and parents.

This chapter also describes four GTL Frameworks: (1) the GTL Framework for Transforming Student Behavior; (2) the GTL Framework for Transforming Student Behavior and Preparing Middle School Students for High School and Life; (3) the GTL Framework for Transforming Student Behavior and Preparing High School Students for College and/or Career and Life; and (4) the GTL Framework for Transforming Parent Relationships and the positive impact they can have on teachers, students, and parents. These frameworks offer guidance to middle school and high school teachers who are working to transform student behavior and parent relationships.

Each GTL Framework is composed of the 11 GTL Word Categories that make up GTL. The GTL Frameworks highlight the power of GTL and the transformational purpose for using GTL. These frameworks serve as a significant starting point for revisiting our teacher language and provide teachers with a reflective model for turning their Language of Practice into GTL.

## Definitions of the 11 Great Teacher Language Word Categories

### Words of Accountability
**Definition for Middle School and High School Students**

*Words of Accountability* call for students to provide an account for their choices. They encourage and remind students that they are responsible to someone or for something. They address a problem "in the moment" and hold students accountable all along the way!

**Goal for Middle Students: Reach personal accountability**
*in middle school and high school and in their future*

**Goal for High School Students: Reach personal accountability**
*in high school and college and/or career and in their life*

**GTL Examples for Middle School and High School Students**

(Whispering to student) "Shouting during class is not a respectful way to communicate that you're bored. I want to better understand why you're feeling bored; let's talk about it after class."

Words of Accountability

(Privately to student) "Because you hit another student, we have to discuss your behavior and your consequences with the principal and your parents. We have school policies to make sure our school is a safe place for everyone, and the school's policy is clear about the consequences for hitting another student."

Words of Accountability

**Definition for Middle School and High School Parents**

*Words of Accountability* provide parents a clear and respectful account of their child's classroom behaviors.

**Goal for Middle School and High School Parents: Parents become well-informed supporters of their child and the teacher**

**GTL Examples for Middle School and High School Parents**

"Since the first day of school, we have been talking about respectful behaviors in our class and the importance of showing respect to one another. We've also discussed how we're going to resolve disrespectful language and behaviors quickly and respectfully to prevent bigger issues from happening. I'm calling you to share something that happened today. Jamie was calling other students disrespectful names and making fun of them during class."

Words of Accountability

"At the beginning of the school year at the Parent Open House, you and I talked about the importance of maintaining a strong relationship and open communication between home and school. That's why I'm calling to share something that happened in class today. Jamie hit another student in our class. The first thing I did was to speak to both students to get an understanding of what happened."

Words of Accountability

## Words of Encouragement
### Definition for Middle School and High School Students

*Words of Encouragement* are specific and supportive words that rally students to overcome fears and failure and to try, try again. These words inspire students with the desire, courage, and confidence to do the right thing for themselves and others. They are words that convey "I believe in you!"

**Goal for Middle Students: Live a better way and become all they can be** *in middle school and high school and in their future*

**Goal for High School Students: Live a better way and become all they can be** *in high school and college and/or career and in their life*

### GTL Examples for Middle School and High School Students

(Privately to the student) "I saw you in the school play last night, and you were amazing! I can see you being an actress one day."

Words of Encouragement

(Privately to student) "I appreciate how you waited to speak and gave the other students your attention while they were speaking. That was very respectful."

Words of Encouragement

### Definition for Middle School and High School Parents

*Words of Encouragement* inspire parents with positive support and encouragement.

### Goal for Middle School and High School Parents: Parents feel encouraged about their child and their child's school experiences

### GTL Examples for Middle School and High School Parents

"Before we finish our conversation, I wanted to share that I have enjoyed having Jamie in my class. He is… (share something personal, positive, and specific that you've experienced with Jamie and link it to a positive quality that could help Jamie in his future in high school or college and/or career and life)."

Words of Encouragement

"I'm calling you to share something great I noticed today at school. Jamie has been so excited about what we are learning in Biology this week. He has been asking questions, sharing information he has learned on his own, and motivating other students to learn more, too."

Words of Encouragement

## Words of Grace
### Definition for Middle School and High School Students

*Words of Grace* demonstrate love, patience, and respect for students despite what they do. They help us acknowledge that "we all make mistakes," "nobody's perfect," and "forgive and forget." These words are not antagonistic, do not harbor ill feelings, and give students another chance to get it right!

### Goal for Middle Students: Experience and practice the power of forgiveness and second chances *in middle school and high school and in their future*

### Goal for High School Students: Experience and practice the power of forgiveness and second chances *in high school and college and/or career and in their life*

## GTL Examples for Middle School and High School Students

(Student returns from an out of school suspension for a blatantly disrespectful act towards you.) "We missed you—I am glad you are back."

Words of Grace

"When someone does something to hurt your feelings, it is important to talk with them about it. Once you have discussed it with them and they have apologized—let's agree to forgive and forget."

Words of Grace

## Definition for Middle School and High School Parents

*Words of Grace* show parents that you offer all students another chance to get it right and forgive their past mistakes.

## Goal for Middle School and High School Parents: Parents see and hear the power of forgiveness and second chances for their child

## GTL Examples for Middle School and High School Parents

"I'm looking forward to meeting with you and working together for Jamie. Although he has not been completing his work, he has plenty of time to catch up and get back on track."

Words of Grace

"Thank you for talking with me today. I want to get to the root of Jamie's behavior and for him to know that I'm not upset with him. However, his behavior today was not acceptable, and hopefully together we can help him avoid that type of behavior in the future."

Words of Grace

## Words of Guidance
### Definition for Middle School and High School Students

*Words of Guidance* give students a positive and supportive path to appropriate behavior, strong character, and success. They offer students advice— "Next time do/try this…Consider this… Here's another way." These words offer students an opportunity to improve and provide direction and assistance to the destination.

**Goal for Middle Students: Practice self-management** *in middle school and high school and in their future*

**Goal for High School Students: Practice self-management** *in high school and college and/or career and in their life*

### GTL Examples for Middle School and High School Students

"As you search for information on today's assignment, let's talk about why it's important for you all to cite the sources you use for your academic work. First of all, citing sources correctly gives credit to the author who wrote or created the information. Second, when you don't cite your sources properly, it miscommunicates to others that you are taking the credit for what someone else has written or created. Third, it miscommunicates to me, your teacher, what you've actually learned about the material and what you've actually written."

Words of Guidance

"You'll have lots of difficult choices to make this year. I want to help you understand that the choices you make matter, and I'll be here to help you with these decisions if you need me. Ultimately, you'll be making the decision and you'll be responsible for your choices."

Words of Guidance

### Definition for Middle School and High School Parents

*Words of Guidance* inform parents of the guidance and assistance that you and the school will provide to their child.

**Goal for Middle School and High School Parents: Parents are confident their child is supported and will receive the personalized guidance and assistance they need throughout the year**

### GTL Examples for Middle School and High School Parents

"We have been discussing the difference between using their cell phones for class lessons or an emergency versus using it for personal texting, video games, listening to music, or social media. Cell phones can be a great tool for learning in class, but they can also be a huge distraction for students' learning. I'm reaching out to you to make you aware of this issue and let you know I'm concerned it could impact Jamie's learning."

Words of Guidance

"My goal is to keep you informed about what we are doing in my course, so you will know what to expect from me and what Jamie will be learning this year. On the school website, you will find our course portal. In that portal, you will find Jamie's weekly assignments and progress updates along with his grades on assignments. You will have access to our course portal throughout the year. Please let me know if you have trouble accessing this information or if you have any questions about it."

Words of Guidance

## Words of High Expectations
### Definition for Middle School and High School Students

*Words of High Expectations* demonstrate a belief in every student's ability to meet the highest levels of personal conduct and success. These words set high expectations and convey the anticipation that all students will meet them. They overcome low expectations and prejudgments. They help students to envision and pursue their best!

**Goal for Middle Students: Achieve their full potential** *in middle school and high school and in their future*

**Goal for High School Students: Achieve their full potential** *in high school and college and/or career and in their life*

**GTL Examples for Middle School and High School Students**

> "I want you all to know I won't expect anything of you that I don't expect from myself. I will make sure I am in class on time, and I will follow our class rules and behavior expectations."
>
> Words of High Expectations

> "Don't be afraid to share your thoughts with the class during our class discussion. We want to hear what you have to say. I know you can do this."
>
> Words of High Expectations

**Definition for Middle School and High School Parents**

*Words of High Expectations* demonstrate to parents how you will help their child envision and pursue their best schoolwork and behavior.

**Goal for Middle School and High School Parents: Parents will expect their child to achieve their full potential both in school and at home**

**GTL Examples for Middle School and High School Parents**

> "As I'm getting to know Jamie this year, I'm going to talk to him about his strengths, hobbies, and interests—so I can encourage him and help him enjoy school and get him thinking about setting goals for high school, college and/or career, and life."
>
> Words of High Expectations

"I can see Jamie having a job in the field of Biology one day."

Words of High Expectations

## Words of Hope

### Definition for Middle School and High School Students

*Words of Hope* inspire us to see others and the world with great potential. These words empower students to dream and achieve more! They instill the confidence that what is hoped for can happen! They also spark interests and ignite passions for learning!

**Goal for Middle Students: Hope for and work for a better tomorrow** *in middle school and high school and in their future*

**Goal for High School Students: Hope for and work for a better tomorrow** *in high school and college and/or career and in their life*

### GTL Examples for Middle School and High School Students

(A student says, 'I'm not doing this—I am dropping out of school when I am 16 anyway.') "It's your choice whether or not you drop out of school, but I'm going to try my best to change your mind and make learning interesting, relevant, and engaging for everyone. I hope my class will be a catalyst for finding your interests and passions so you can find a great job when you graduate."

Words of Hope

"You look frustrated. Let's talk about what's frustrating you today, and we can decide how to work through this problem together so it won't frustrate you tomorrow."

Words of Hope

### Definition for Middle School and High School Parents

*Words of Hope* inspire parents to look beyond the current circumstances and expect greater things for their child.

### Goal for Middle School and High School Parents: Parents experience ongoing hope for their child throughout the school year

### GTL Examples for Middle School and High School Parents

"I'm calling you to share some great news about Jamie and how he's been doing in class. He's been coming into class and getting right to work quietly and quickly. His improved behavior is also paying off with improved grades, and I was excited to share it with you!"

Words of Hope

"As I mentioned to you earlier, Jamie has a lot of potential and I can imagine him using his personality and strengths to be whatever he wants to be in his future. I really want to make sure we're doing everything we—you, Jamie, and I—can to address these class disruptions so he can experience success now and in his future."

Words of Hope

## Words of Love
### Definition for Middle School and High School Students

*Words of Love* demonstrate an awareness that everyone needs to be loved, cared for, and valued. These words inspire students to use their words, talents, and gifts to help others. These words of love should never be confused with a "romantic love" nor should they be without accountability. Instead, these words are caring and supportive *with* accountability—the foundation for a strong relationship. They demonstrate the patience to endure students' misbehavior and an unwavering commitment and belief that students can improve!

### Goal for Middle Students: Experience and practice the selfless power and purpose of putting others first *in middle school and high school and in their future*

**Goal for High School Students: Experience and practice the selfless power and purpose of putting others first** *in high school and college and/or career and in their life*

### GTL Examples for Middle School and High School Students

> (Shared with the whole class) "When anger happens in our class, I don't want to respond to anyone's anger with my own anger. My goal is to stay calm and focus on how to help you work through your anger."
>
> Words of Love

> (Shared with the whole class) "I care about all of you, and I want you all to be successful in life, so I'm going to hold each of you accountable for the choices you make."
>
> Words of Love

### Definition for Middle School and High School Parents

**Words of Love** touch parents' hearts and demonstrate love and care for them and their child unconditionally.

**Goal for Middle School and High School Parents: Parents know without a doubt their child will experience unconditional care and receive loving accountability throughout the year**

### GTL Examples for Middle School and High School Parents

> "I spoke with Jamie in private to find out if he was feeling OK. I wanted to make sure he wasn't sick or needed to go see the school nurse or call home."
>
> Words of Love

> "Jamie and your family are very important to me. If you can think of anything we can do to make things better for Jamie this year, please let me know."
>
> Words of Love

## Words of Relationship

### Definition for Middle School and High School Students

*Words of Relationship* help to maintain an emotionally safe and secure environment where students trust you and know where they stand. These words demonstrate a desire to relate to students and to work with them to break down walls, build bridges, and reach common ground! They establish and nurture meaningful bonds with students by showing them they are "worth it"—they are valued and worth your time and your effort! Use these words when you talk with students individually—"heart to heart."

**Goal for Middle Students: Develop positive lifelong relationships with others** *in middle school and high school and in their future*

**Goal for High School Students: Develop positive lifelong relationships with others** *in high school and college and/or career and in their life*

### GTL Examples for Middle School and High School Students

(Shared privately to help a consistently tardy student to feel connected to your class) "I was wondering if you would be interested in helping me lead a discussion tomorrow in class? I'll provide the questions you will ask the other students."

Words of Relationship

(One-on-one conversation with student) "I noticed during break you were listening to music. What do you listen to? What do you like?"

Words of Relationship

### Definition for Middle School and High School Parents

**Words of Relationship** establish a trusting, caring, respectful, and positive connection with every parent.

**Goal for Middle School and High School Parents: Parents experience the power of a positive and transformational relationship with you and the school**

**GTL Examples for Middle School and High School Parents**

"Jamie has such a natural curiosity about Biology, and he is always so engaged in Biology class. He's a great role model for the other students in our class. I am proud of him and his desire to learn."
Words of Relationship

"At the beginning of the school year at the Parent Open House, we talked about the importance of maintaining a strong relationship and open communication between home and school. That's why I called today to share this update about Jamie."
Words of Relationship

## Words of Respect
### Definition for Middle School and High School Students

*Words of Respect* demonstrate a proper regard for the dignity of one's character and the character of others. These words convey an intentional and careful consideration and appreciation of others. Words of respect acknowledge the value of all people.

**Goal for Middle Students: Model respect for self and others** *in middle school and high school and in their future*

**Goal for High School Students: Model respect for self and others** *in high school and college and/or career and in their life*

**GTL Examples for Middle School and High School Students**

"We are not always going to agree, but when we have disagreements, we owe each other respect."
Words of Respect

(Whispering to student) "I don't want to single you out in front of everybody, but we need to talk after class about your behavior just now."

Words of Respect

### Definition for Middle School and High School Parents

**Words of Respect** demonstrate an intentional consideration and appreciation for all parents.

### Goal for Middle School and High School Parents: Parents feel respected and valued by you

### GTL Examples for Middle School and High School Parents

"Hello! My name is…. I'm Jamie's teacher. He's not in trouble. Is now a good time for us to talk?"

Words of Respect

"I also want to share my contact information with you (share your school contact information) and let you know I'm available to answer any questions or concerns you have this year. I look forward to working with you and getting to know you this year."

Words of Respect

## Words of Understanding
### Definition for Middle School and High School Students

*Words of Understanding* demonstrate a conscious and deliberate effort to understand someone else's perspective by putting yourself in their position, putting yourself in their shoes, seeing things through their eyes, and hearing things through their ears. When individual student issues arise, these words demonstrate the desire to truly understand "what's going on" with the student by asking thoughtful questions that get to the root of the problem.

**Goal for Middle Students: Experience and practice empathy for others** *in middle school and high school and in their future*

**Goal for High School Students: Experience and practice empathy for others** *in high school and college and/or career and in their life*

### GTL Examples for Middle School and High School Students

(A student continuously says, "I am not going to do this work.") "Can you help me understand what it is about this work that keeps you from doing it? Is it too hard, too easy, are you not interested in it? Let's take some time now to work out a plan for helping you to do your work in this class."

Words of Understanding

(Privately to the verbally disrespectful student) "Help me understand how you were feeling just now. Were you angry at me or someone? I want to understand."

Words of Understanding

### Definition for Middle School and High School Parents

**Words of Understanding** demonstrate your desire to truly understand the parents' perspective.

**Goal for Middle School and High School Parents: Parents are heard, understood, and valued as vital partners in ensuring their child's success**

### GTL Examples for Middle School and High School Parents

"I talked with Jamie to get an understanding about his behavior. I wanted him to know that I think he is very capable of doing the work and that I'm here to help him when it gets challenging."

Words of Understanding

"So I wanted to reach out and make you aware of his behavior and work together to get to the bottom of what is going on with Jamie. Has Jamie shared anything with you about our class, or other students in our class, that could give us a better understanding of how he's feeling about school? If he shares more with you while he's home, please let me know. I really want to understand what caused this and how to keep it from happening again."

Words of Understanding

## Words of Unity

### Definition for Students

*Words of Unity* transform a group of individuals into a team culture. These words encourage a "sense of belonging" and make it clear to all students that their presence and participation in classroom activities are valuable to the team. They also establish and promote a network of support in the classroom and beyond.

### Goal for Middle Students: Practice transformational teamwork through collaboration, agreement, and cooperation
*in middle school and high school and in their future*

### Goal for High School Students: Practice transformational teamwork through collaboration, agreement, and cooperation
*in high school and college and/or career and in their life*

### GTL Examples for Students

"That's an interesting way to think about it—I've never thought about it that way. I don't agree with you, but in order for us to move ahead in our lesson, we need to agree to disagree for now."

Words of Unity

"Today, we are going to work together to develop our classroom rules, behavior expectations, and group work norms for our classroom. We'll also discuss our school's policies and why they are important. It's important that everyone have an opportunity to share their thoughts and ideas."

Words of Unity

### Definition for Parents

**Words of Unity** create a transformational culture of collaboration and teamwork with all parents.

**Goal for Middle School and High School Parents: Parents become personally engaged members of your classroom team**

### GTL Examples for Parents

"Today in class, we worked together to develop our rules and behavior expectations for our class, and we created an agreement page for students, parents, and me to sign. Jamie will bring it home for you to sign and return to school. Our goal is for everybody to understand and agree on these rules and behavior expectations."

Words of Unity

"I've been talking to Jamie and working with him individually, and I also need your insight and influence and help. Could we meet sometime this week and sit down together to design the support plan for Jamie? Together, we can get him the support he needs to be successful."

Words of Unity

### The Four Great Teacher Language Frameworks for Transforming Student Behavior and Parent Relationships in Middle School and High School

### The Great Teacher Language Framework for Transforming Student Behavior in the Classroom and Beyond

Table 2.1 presents the GTL Framework for Transforming Student Behavior in the Classroom and Beyond. This GTL framework has

**Table 2.1** The Great Teacher Language Framework for Transforming Student Behavior in the Classroom and Beyond

| Instead of | Use | To | So That Students |
|---|---|---|---|
| Allowing students to be irresponsible | Words of Accountability | Hold them accountable all along the way | Reach personal accountability. |
| Unintentionally allowing students to become discouraged | Words of Encouragement | Rally students with the courage to overcome challenges, obstacles, barriers, failures, defeats, fears, apathy, and so on | Live a better way and become all they can be. |
| Harboring ill feelings like unforgiveness and blame | Words of Grace | Separate the student from the behavior, forgive their past mistakes, and give them another chance to get it right | Experience and practice the power of forgiveness and second chances. |
| Hoping that students find their way | Words of Guidance | Help students find a path to success and appropriate behavior | Practice self-management. |
| Unintentionally discouraging and limiting students with low expectations | Words of High Expectations | Help students envision and pursue their best | Achieve their full potential. |
| Surviving for today | Words of Hope | Inspire a vision of a better tomorrow | Hope for and work for a better tomorrow. |

| | | | |
|---|---|---|---|
| Speaking only to the minds of students | *Words of Love* | Touch their hearts and demonstrate love and care unconditionally | Experience and practice the selfless power and purpose of putting others first. |
| Focusing only on the course content | *Words of Relationship* | Establish a caring and positive connection with each student | Develop positive lifelong relationships with others. |
| Allowing a climate of disrespect in your classroom | *Words of Respect* | Demonstrate a mutual admiration for one another | Model respect for self and others. |
| Making assumptions based upon your perspective | *Words of Understanding* | Discover the student's perspective | Experience and practice empathy for others. |
| Doing everything by yourself | *Words of Unity* | Nurture a culture of collaboration and teamwork in your classroom | Practice transformational teamwork through collaboration, agreement, and cooperation. |

four columns and 11 rows. Each row represents the transformational impacts of using the GTL Word Categories with students.

The first column is the "Instead of" column. The "Instead of" column describes teacher behaviors that are sometimes used in the classroom. However, these "Instead of" behaviors often result in teacher and/or student frustration, unproductive outcomes, short-term solutions, or teacher and student burnout.

The second column, the anchor of the framework, is the "Use" column. The "Use" column lists the 11 GTL Word Categories that can lead to transformational outcomes with students. These 11 GTL Word Categories provide a bridge between the "Instead of" column and the "To" column. For example, "Instead of" unintentionally allowing students to become discouraged, "Use" Words of Encouragement "To" rally students with the courage to overcome challenges, obstacles, barriers, failures, defeats, fears, apathy, and so on.

The third column is the "To" column. The "To" column describes great teacher behaviors and transformational practices to use with students! For example, great teachers "Use" Words of Guidance "To" help students find a path to success and appropriate behavior.

The fourth column of the framework is the "So That Students" column. The "So That Students" column describes the student behavior goals and the student behavior transformations that are possible when we use GTL! For example, "Instead of" harboring ill feelings like unforgiveness and blame, "Use" Words of Grace "To" separate the student from the behavior, forgive their past mistakes, and give them a second chance to get it right "So that Students" experience and practice the power of forgiveness and second chances!

### The Great Teacher Language Framework for Transforming Student Behavior and Preparing Middle School Students for High School and Life

Table 2.2 presents the GTL Framework for Transforming Student Behavior and Preparing Middle School Students for High School and Life. This GTL framework has four columns

Table 2.2 Great Teacher Language Framework for Transforming Student Behavior and Preparing **Middle School Students** for High School and Life

| Instead of | Use | To | So That Middle School Students |
|---|---|---|---|
| Allowing middle school students to be irresponsible | Words of Accountability | Hold them accountable all along the way | Reach personal accountability in middle school and high school and in their future. |
| Unintentionally allowing middle school students to become discouraged | Words of Encouragement | Rally students with the courage to overcome challenges, obstacles, barriers, failures, defeats, fears, apathy, and so on | Live a better way and become all they can be in middle school and high school and in their future. |
| Harboring ill feelings like unforgiveness and blame | Words of Grace | Separate the student from the behavior, forgive their past mistakes, and give them another chance to get it right | Experience and practice the power of forgiveness and second chances in middle school and high school and in their future. |
| Hoping that middle school students find their way | Words of Guidance | Help students find a path to success and appropriate behavior | Practice self-management in middle school and high school and in their future. |
| Unintentionally discouraging and limiting middle school students with low expectations | Words of High Expectations | Help students envision and pursue their best | Achieve their full potential in middle school and high school and in their future. |
| Surviving for today | Words of Hope | Inspire a vision of a better tomorrow | Hope for and work for a better tomorrow in middle school and high school and in their future. |

(Continued)

**Table 2.2** (Continued)

| Instead of | Use | To | So That Middle School Students |
|---|---|---|---|
| Speaking only to the minds of middle school students | Words of Love | Touch their hearts and demonstrate love and care unconditionally | Experience and practice the selfless power and purpose of putting others first in middle school and high school and in their future. |
| Focusing only on the course content | Words of Relationship | Establish a caring and positive connection with each student | Develop positive lifelong relationships with others in middle school and high school and in their future. |
| Allowing a climate of disrespect in your classroom | Words of Respect | Demonstrate a mutual admiration for one another | Model respect for self and others in middle school and high school and in their future. |
| Making assumptions based upon your perspective | Words of Understanding | Discover the student's perspective | Experience and practice empathy for others in middle school and high school and in their future. |
| Doing everything by yourself | Words of Unity | Nurture a culture of collaboration and teamwork in your classroom | Practice transformational teamwork through collaboration, agreement, and cooperation in middle school and high school and in their future. |

and 11 rows. Each row represents the transformational impacts of using the GTL Word Categories with middle school students.

The first column is the "Instead of" column. The "Instead of" column describes teacher behaviors that are sometimes used in the classroom. However, these "Instead of" behaviors often result in teacher and/or student frustration, unproductive outcomes, short-term solutions, or teacher and student burnout.

The second column, the anchor of the framework, is the "Use" column. The "Use" column lists the 11 GTL Word Categories that can lead to transformational outcomes with middle school students. These 11 GTL Word Categories provide a bridge between the "Instead of" column and the "To" column. For example, "Instead of" unintentionally allowing middle school students to become discouraged, "Use" Words of Encouragement "To" rally students with the courage to overcome challenges, obstacles, barriers, failures, defeats, fears, apathy, and so on.

The third column is the "To" column. The "To" column describes great teacher behaviors and transformational practices to use with middle school students! For example, great teachers "Use" Words of Guidance "To" help students find a path to success and appropriate behavior.

The fourth column of the framework is the "So That Middle School Students" column. This column describes the middle school student behavior goals and behavior transformations that are possible when we use GTL! For example, "Instead of" harboring ill feelings like unforgiveness and blame, "Use" Words of Grace "To" separate the student from the behavior, forgive their past mistakes, and give them a second chance to get it right "So that Middle School Students" experience and practice the power of forgiveness and second chances in middle school and high school and in their future!

**The Great Teacher Language Framework for Transforming Student Behavior and Preparing High School Students for College and/or Career and Life**

Table 2.3 presents the GTL Framework for Transforming Student Behavior and Preparing High School Students for College and/or Career and Life. This GTL framework has four columns and 11 rows. Each row represents the transformational

**Table 2.3** Great Teacher Language Framework for Transforming Student Behavior and Preparing **High School Students** for College and/or Career and Life

| Instead of | Use | To | So That High School Students |
|---|---|---|---|
| Allowing high school students to be irresponsible | *Words of Accountability* | Hold them accountable all along the way | Reach personal accountability in high school and college and/or career and in their life. |
| Unintentionally allowing high school students to become discouraged | *Words of Encouragement* | Rally students with the courage to overcome challenges, obstacles, barriers, failures, defeats, fears, apathy, and so on | Live a better way and become all they can be in high school and college and/or career and in their life. |
| Harboring ill feelings like unforgiveness and blame | *Words of Grace* | Separate the student from the behavior; forgive their past mistakes, and give them another chance to get it right | Experience and practice the power of forgiveness and second chances in high school and college and/or career and in their life. |
| Hoping that high school students find their way | *Words of Guidance* | Help students find a path to success and appropriate behavior | Practice self-management in high school and college and/or career and in their life. |
| Unintentionally discouraging and limiting high school students with low expectations | *Words of High Expectations* | Help students envision and pursue their best | Achieve their full potential in high school and college and/or career and in their life. |

## The 11 Great Teacher Language Word Categories and Frameworks ◆ 33

| | | |
|---|---|---|
| Surviving for today | *Words of Hope* — Inspire a vision of a better tomorrow | Hope for and work for a better tomorrow in high school and college and/or career and in their life. |
| Speaking only to the minds of high school students | *Words of Love* — Touch their hearts and demonstrate love and care unconditionally | Experience and practice the selfless power and purpose of putting others first in high school and college and/or career and in their life. |
| Focusing only on the course content | *Words of Relationship* — Establish a caring and positive connection with each student | Develop positive lifelong relationships with others in high school and college and/or career and in their life. |
| Allowing a climate of disrespect in your classroom | *Words of Respect* — Demonstrate a mutual admiration for one another | Model respect for self and others in high school and college and/or career and in their life. |
| Making assumptions based upon your perspective | *Words of Understanding* — Discover the student's perspective | Experience and practice empathy for others in high school and college and/or career and in their life. |
| Doing everything by yourself | *Words of Unity* — Nurture a culture of collaboration and teamwork in your classroom | Practice transformational teamwork through collaboration, agreement, and cooperation in high school and college and/or career and in their life. |

impacts of using the GTL Word Categories with high school students.

The first column is the "Instead of" column. The "Instead of" column describes teacher behaviors that are sometimes used in the classroom. However, these "Instead of" behaviors often result in teacher and/or student frustration, unproductive outcomes, short-term solutions, or teacher and student burnout.

The second column, the anchor of the framework, is the "Use" column. The "Use" column lists the 11 GTL Word Categories that can lead to transformational outcomes with high school students. These 11 GTL Word Categories provide a bridge between the "Instead of" column and the "To" column. For example, "Instead of" unintentionally allowing high school students to become discouraged, "Use" Words of Encouragement "To" rally students with the courage to overcome challenges, obstacles, barriers, failures, defeats, fears, apathy, and so on.

The third column is the "To" column. The "To" column describes great teacher behaviors and transformational practices to use with high school students! For example, great teachers "Use" Words of Guidance "To" help students find a path to success and appropriate behavior.

The fourth column of the framework is the "So That High School Students" column. This column describes the high school student behavior goals and behavior transformations that are possible when we use GTL! For example, "Instead of" harboring ill feelings like unforgiveness and blame, "Use" Words of Grace "To" separate the student from the behavior, forgive their past mistakes, and give them a second chance to get it right "So that High School Students" experience and practice the power of forgiveness and second chances in high school and college and/or career and in their life!

**The Great Teacher Language Framework for Transforming Parent Relationships**

Table 2.4 presents the GTL Framework for Transforming Parent Relationships. This GTL framework has four columns and 11 rows. Each row represents the transformational impacts of using the GTL Word Categories with parents.

The 11 Great Teacher Language Word Categories and Frameworks ◆ 35

**Table 2.4** The Great Teacher Language Framework for Transforming Parent Relationships

| Instead of | Use | To | So That Middle School and High School Parents |
|---|---|---|---|
| Allowing parents to be uninformed or misinformed about classroom issues | Words of Accountability | Provide parents a clear and respectful account of their child's classroom behaviors | Become well-informed supporters of their child and the teacher. |
| Unintentionally allowing parents to become discouraged | Words of Encouragement | Inspire parents with positive support and encouragement | Feel encouraged about their child and their child's school experiences now and in their future. |
| Allowing parents to experience a classroom culture of unforgiveness and blame | Words of Grace | Show parents that you offer all students another chance to get it right and forgive their past mistakes | See and hear the power of forgiveness and second chances for their child. |
| Hoping parents find the guidance and assistance they need to support their child's success | Words of Guidance | Inform parents of the guidance and assistance that you and the school will provide to their child | Are confident their child is supported and will receive the personalized guidance and assistance they need throughout the year and for their child's future success. |
| Discouraging parents by having low expectations for their child | Words of High Expectations | Demonstrate to parents how you will help their child envision and pursue their best schoolwork and behavior | Will expect their child to achieve their full potential both in school and at home and in their future. |

(Continued)

**Table 2.4** (Continued)

| Instead of | Use | To | So That Middle School and High School Parents |
|---|---|---|---|
| Allowing parents to feel discouraged about their child's current school situation | Words of Hope | Inspire parents to look beyond the current circumstances and expect greater things for their child | Experience ongoing hope for their child throughout the school year and for their future. |
| Speaking only to the minds of parents | Words of Love | Touch parents' hearts and demonstrate love and care for them and their child unconditionally | Know without a doubt their child will experience unconditional care and receive loving accountability throughout the year. |
| Focusing only on providing parents with facts and information | Words of Relationship | Establish a trusting, caring, respectful, and positive connection with every parent | Experience the power of a positive and transformational relationship with you and the school. |
| Responding to parents disrespectfully | Words of Respect | Demonstrate an intentional consideration and appreciation for all parents | Feel respected and valued by you. |
| Making assumptions about parents based on your perspective | Words of Understanding | Demonstrate your desire to truly understand the parents' perspective | Are heard, understood, and valued as vital partners in ensuring their child's success now and in their future. |
| Doing everything by yourself, without parents | Words of Unity | Create a transformational culture of collaboration and teamwork with all parents | Become personally engaged members of your school community. |

The first column is the "Instead of" column. The "Instead of" column describes teacher behaviors that are sometimes used with parents. However, these "Instead of" behaviors often result in teacher and/or parent frustration, unproductive outcomes, short-term solutions, or teacher and parent burnout.

The second column, the anchor of the framework, is the "Use" column. The "Use" column lists the 11 GTL Word Categories that can lead to transformational outcomes with parents. These 11 GTL Word Categories provide a bridge between the "Instead of" column and the "To" column. For example, "Instead of" unintentionally allowing parents to become discouraged, "Use" Words of Encouragement "To" inspire parents with positive support and encouragement.

The third column is the "To" column. The "To" column describes great teacher behaviors and transformational practices to use with parents! For example, great teachers "Use" Words of Guidance "To" inform parents of the guidance and assistance that you and the school will provide their child.

The fourth column of the framework is the "So That Middle School and High School Parents" column. The "So That Middle School and High School Parents" column describes the parent relationship goals and relationship transformations that are possible when we use GTL! For example, "Instead of" allowing parents to experience a classroom culture of unforgiveness and blame, "Use" Words of Grace "To" show parents that you offer all students another chance to get it right and forgive their past mistakes "So that Middle School and High School Parents" see and hear the power of forgiveness and second chances for their child!

## The Great Teacher Language Frameworks for Transformation

The more you use these GTL Frameworks and integrate these GTL Word Categories and GTL examples into your daily teaching practice and make them your own, the more you will be able to transform student behavior, parent relationships, and your classroom culture.

Chapter 3 strategically focuses on GTL you can use on the first day of school and the days that follow with students and parents. Chapters 4 through 10 present challenging classroom behavior scenarios. Each chapter begins with the question 'What Do Great Teachers Say?' and identifies four to eight specific student behavior scenarios that are common in today's middle school and high school classrooms. In each chapter, you'll also find relevant and helpful background information related to each classroom behavior scenario. All of these chapters offer teacher-friendly charts with *GTL Reminders to Self, GTL to Share with Students, GTL to Use When Talking and Communicating with Parents*, and *GTL Whole Class Activities*. At the end of the book, we have included an *Index of GTL Student Behavior Scenarios* that lists the 42 student behavior scenarios in Chapters 4 through 10.

# 3
# What Do Great Teachers Say on the First Day of School and the Days that Follow?

It's the first day of school and you're excited to meet your new students and learn with them. This first day of middle school or high school and the days that follow give you an opportunity to get to know them, for them to get to know you, and for the students to get to know each other. This chapter provides teacher-friendly charts with Great Teacher Language (GTL) Reminders to Self, GTL to Share with Students, GTL to Use When Talking and Communicating with Parents, and GTL Classroom Activities specifically related to the following six Great Classroom Culture Behavior Standards:

- Standard 3.1: Setting High Expectations for All
- Standard 3.2: Establishing the Rules and Behavior Expectations for Success
- Standard 3.3: Creating a Culture of Community and Teamwork
- Standard 3.4: Encouraging Life-Long Self-Management
- Standard 3.5: Leading by Example
- Standard 3.6: Building Relationships with Students and Their Families

> We know these are not the only classroom behavior standards that you will communicate to your students on the first day of school and the days that follow. These specific classroom behavior standards are a starting point for you to develop your GTL for your classroom on the first day and every day. It is important for you to share with your middle school or high school students how these classroom behavior standards will positively impact them now and in their future. For some of our classroom behavior standards, we have included GTL examples for you to use when talking and communicating with parents. These GTL examples are templates for phone conversations, emails, or other types of messages to develop strong communication between teachers and parents and to promote understanding, relationships, trust, and collaboration.

On the first day of school with a classroom full of middle school or high school students, your words can make all the difference. Some students are excited about what's in store; others are nervous and anxious; while others were perfectly happy with their summer vacation and are now quite disappointed and seem apathetic about being back in school. Acknowledging and addressing these first-day feelings of excitement, anxiety, fear, uncertainty about their future, disappointment about being back in school, and overall general apathy are perhaps a teacher's first challenge—or opportunity—to connect with each student on a personal level. A teacher's Language of Practice (LoP) in the form of GTL during these first days sets the tone, provides direction, and conveys expectations of what is to come. These initial words embody the teacher's beliefs and values and provide an example of what the teacher expects to see and hear from all students. Your GTL establishes standards and structures that promote a safe and secure environment, both physically and emotionally, and can offer your new students the accountability, encouragement, grace, guidance, high expectations, hope, love, relationships, respect, understanding, and unity they need to begin and continue the best school year yet.

## Setting High Expectations for All

Setting high expectations for middle school and high school students begins on the first day of school. The high expectations that teachers convey to all their students can propel each of them closer to reaching their potential. What if these high expectations are presented without encouragement and clear guidance? Sometimes students hear high expectations but don't have a personal map or the tools to get there. Telling students "You can do anything you set your mind to" or "You can be anything you want to be" can be confusing for a student who has never experienced academic success or who has a discipline folder full of past mistakes. This confusion can be addressed with a consistent language that offers real hope with real guidance. What do you expect of your students? What do you want your students to expect of you? How will you offer encouragement and guidance to help students reach their potential in middle school and high school and in their future?

The following GTL examples offer words that teachers can use on their first day of school and in the days that follow to set high expectations for both students and themselves. Within these language examples, you will find GTL Words of Encouragement, Words of Grace, Words of Guidance, Words of Hope, Words of Relationship, and Words of Unity. Weaving these additional GTL words into your Words of High Expectations can provide the support your students need to reach their potential this year and in the future.

---

### WHAT DO GREAT TEACHERS SAY WHEN…?

**Setting High Expectations for All (Classroom Behavior Standard 3.1)**

#### GTL Reminders to Self:

*Remember…* To keep you and your students encouraged in your classroom, provide daily opportunities for students to be successful.

Words of Encouragement

*Remember…* Have high expectations for every student who walks through your door.
Words of High Expectations

*Remember…* Hope brings energy to students and to the teacher.
Words of Hope

*Remember…* Setting high expectations for your students begins on the first day of school.
Words of Guidance

*Remember…* Offer each student a fresh start to their new school year.
Words of Grace

*Remember…* There is wisdom in reviewing a student's past academic and behavior records, but don't let their past mistakes define them this year.
Words of Grace

### GTL to Share with Students:

"This year we are going to be learning some difficult things, and I am excited about helping each of you learn as much as you can. If you're thinking you won't learn in my course, I'm going to work hard to change your mind!"
Words of Encouragement

"The 'not so good' things you did in the past don't have to affect what you do this year. We are all going to have a new start!"
Words of Grace

"Each of you has strengths and talents. As I get to know you this year, I'm here to help you discover them and use them to do well this year."
Words of Guidance

"I am so excited about this new school year. I have always loved school, and I have always loved to learn. My hope is that I can share my love of learning with you!"
Words of Hope

"I expect a lot from each of you, and I want you all to expect a lot from me. Let's talk about what you expect from me as your teacher."
Words of High Expectations

"We're going to need to work together to make this a great school year for everyone."
Words of Unity

"I am committed to making our lessons interesting and relevant to all of you. My goal is to help each of you make a personal connection to what we're learning."
Words of Relationship

"We all need encouragement. I need it. Let's remember to encourage each other with our words and actions."
Words of Encouragement

"I encourage you all to have goals and dreams. My hope for all of you is that you dare to have dreams and work hard to achieve them."
Words of Hope

## Establishing the Rules and Behavior Expectations for Success

On the first day of school, it is essential that you establish rules and behavior expectations with your middle school and high school students. As you and your students discuss (1) possible rules for your classroom, (2) what they expect of you as their teacher, and (3) what you can expect of them as students, it is important to involve all the students and value everyone's input. Student-generated behavior expectations for both the teacher and themselves—supported with teacher guidance—can almost guarantee student buy-in and a classroom culture that offers support for student success now and in the future.

The rules and expectations for classroom behavior that you and your students decide on together and the language used in your classroom will generate your classroom culture. Providing students with clear language examples of Words of Accountability, Words of Encouragement, Words of Grace, Words of Guidance, Words of High Expectations, Words of Hope, Words of Love, Words of Relationship, Words of Respect, Words of Understanding, and Words of Unity offers students an idea of how they can respond appropriately to situations before, during, and after they encounter them.

In fact, our hope is that middle schools and high schools provide the structure and guidelines that students need to practice self-management in school, in the real world, and in their future. What will the rules and behavior expectations "sound like" in your classroom? How will you facilitate a classroom rules, school policies, and behavior expectations discussion that respects everyone's input and also incorporates your values and beliefs? How do you plan to encourage input from all students? What will you say if a student suggests an inappropriate rule? (At the end of this chapter, see the GTL Classroom Activity entitled "Hit the Pause Button Introduction for Setting up Teacher and Student Behavior Expectations, Classroom Rules, Group Work Norms, and Discussing School Policies".)

The first day of school is such a "blank slate." Our words are so important in creating and developing teacher and student behavior expectations, classroom rules, and explaining school policies. Below are GTL examples to guide you and your students as you develop the teacher and student behavior expectations and rules on the first day of school.

## WHAT DO GREAT TEACHERS SAY WHEN…?

**Establishing Rules and Behavior Expectations for Success (Classroom Behavior Standard 3.2)**

### GTL Reminders to Self:

*Remember…* Creating your rules and behavior expectations in a positive and collaborative way will ensure buy-in from your students.

Words of Love

*Remember…* Students do not need to guess what is right or wrong in your classroom. From Day 1, they need to know what the rules, behavior expectations, group work norms, and school policies are. They also need to hear from you why these policies are important.

Words of High Expectations

*Remember…* From the very first day of class, encourage students to have ownership in your classroom by working as a team to set up the classroom rules, behavior expectations, and group work norms and to participate in a collaborative discussion about their school's policies.

Words of Unity

*Remember…* During the first day of school, ask your students to write their expectations of you as their teacher on Post-it notes.

Words of High Expectations

*Remember…* Distractions and misbehaviors can mess up your lesson plan. It is important to "hit the pause button" on the lesson and seize opportunities to address these behaviors immediately by talking with the whole class about the issue. Addressing the misbehavior immediately may solve the discipline issue for the rest of the school year and sets the tone for your classroom behavior expectations.

See the GTL Classroom Activities (Hit the Pause Button) at the end of Chapters 4 to 10 for examples.

Words of Accountability

**GTL to Share with Students:**

"Today we are going to work together to develop our classroom rules, behavior expectations, and group work norms for our classroom. We'll also discuss our school's policies and why they are important. It's important that everyone have an opportunity to share their thoughts and ideas."

Words of Unity

"Let's talk about the rules, behavior expectations, and group work norms for our classroom this year and our school's policies. Once we all agree on these rules, behavior expectations, group work norms, and school policies, I will ask your parents to sign that they agree with them. Then we will all be on the same page. I'm looking forward to working with you and your parents this year."

Words of Unity

"It's important for all of you to know that I am going to hold everyone accountable to the same rules, behavior expectations, and group work norms and our school policies."

Words of Accountability

"Our classroom rules, behavior expectations, group work norms, and school policies will help us get along better in school, outside of school, and in the future."

Words of Guidance

"From time to time this year, I am going to have personal conferences with you. These conferences will be opportunities for you to share problems or concerns you have, and we can discuss what we can do together to help you be successful."
Words of Guidance

"Now that we've agreed on our rules, behavior expectations, and group work norms, let's talk about what each of these would 'sound like and look like?' What does respecting each other sound like and look like?"
Words of Respect

"Before we move on, let's make sure that everyone understands what we have discussed. Does anyone have any questions about the rules, behavior expectations, group work norms, and school policies we have discussed and agreed on today?"
Words of Understanding

"I want all of you to feel comfortable in this class. We have procedures and clear expectations to keep our classroom a safe place for all of us to learn."
Words of Unity

"You can expect me to treat all of you with respect and care."
Words of Love

## Creating a Culture of Community and Teamwork

Your GTL on the first day of school and the days that follow will lay the foundation for relationship building, team building, school pride, trust, and mutual respect. Creating a Great Classroom Culture of community and teamwork begins with a teacher who says, "I am willing to listen to you, and I want to know what you think." When middle school and high school students know their voices are heard and valued, they feel connected—like they belong to something. Student input in the development of the classroom culture leads to unity, empowerment, a sense of belonging, teamwork, and collaboration. What classroom culture do you believe will be the most conducive to students' academic success and social maturity? Are you willing to encourage feedback and input from your students? How will your language encourage all students to be part of the team?

Below are GTL examples to guide you and your students as you work together to create a culture of community and teamwork on the first day of school, in the days that follow, and in their future.

---

### WHAT DO GREAT TEACHERS SAY WHEN...?

**Creating a Culture of Community and Teamwork (Classroom Behavior Standard 3.3)**

#### GTL Reminders to Self:

*Remember...* Your classroom needs to be a place where students thrive, not just survive.

Words of Hope

*Remember...* Your job as a teacher is much like a musical conductor blending each individual student note into something harmonious.

Words of Unity

*Remember...* When students feel like they belong to something—in this case, the smaller classroom community and the larger school community—they are more likely to work together as a team.

Words of Unity

*Remember...* There is a big difference between asking a student to do something and telling a student to do something. Asking students to be part of the team demonstrates a level of respect; on the other hand, telling them they are going to be on the team suggests a demand.

Words of Respect

*Remember…* Instead of always saying 'No' to students who want to do something at an inappropriate time, consider a 'Yes with Guidance'. For example, when a group of students wants to go to the media center to work on a project, instead of saying "No, now is not the time to go to the media center", say "Yes, your group can go when we finish this activity."

Words of Guidance

### GTL to Share with Students:

"Now that we have discussed and decided on the rules and behavior expectations for our class, let's move on. I'm excited to start today's lesson."

Words of Encouragement

"We all make mistakes. At some point this year, everybody in this class—including me—will do something that causes us to feel embarrassed. Let's agree not to make fun of others and laugh at them when this happens, because that will make them feel more embarrassed."

Words of Respect

"When a new student joins our class, let's respect them and welcome them."

Words of Respect

"My job is to teach you as much as I can this year, but I see myself as a life-long learner, too. I know there will be many times when I will learn a lot from you and what you have to share."

Words of Relationship

"This year we are going to have class meetings. These meetings will be an opportunity for us to discuss problems, work together to come up with solutions, and prevent them from happening."
Words of Unity

"We have behavior expectations and group norms for doing group projects in our class. The goal is to maximize the time in your groups. Are there any questions?"
Words of Guidance

"Let's work together to develop a list of the class goals for this year and another list for what we need to do to make them happen."
Words of Unity

"If we have problems or issues in our class, we are going to talk and work together to reach a solution so in the end everyone is saying 'Yes, that was a good way to solve that problem.'"
Words of Unity

"In our class, we don't want anyone to feel embarrassed to ask questions or share their ideas. Let's work together to respect each other's thoughts and ideas, so everyone feels confident to share."
Words of Respect

"We want everyone to be proud of our school and feel like they're part of a team. In our school and in our class, we are a team. We'll support each other, motivate each other, see things through others' eyes, hear things through others' ears, and respect each other."
Words of Unity

"We all agreed in our classroom conversation last week on how we will handle this specific problem we're having. So let's follow through with the decision we made together."
Words of Accountability

## Encouraging Life-Long Self-Management

Encouraging your middle school and high school students and guiding them to become self-managed people starts on the first day of school. When students learn to become self-managed, they choose to manage their own behavior without coercion or control from others. When we use our power and authority to coerce students into doing something, it might provide a short-term, quick fix in your classroom now, but it doesn't persuade or empower students to choose to manage their own behavior in the moment or for their lifetime. Teacher language in the form of GTL sets the stage for an environment that helps students move from a mindset where "The teacher's trying to make me do this" to "I'm doing this because I'm choosing to do it, and it's the right thing to do."

It is also important to promote a classroom environment where students understand that they have the freedom to choose their behaviors. Along with that freedom, however, they will have to accept responsibility for those choices and realize the impact their choices have on themselves, their future, and the people around them. (At the end of this chapter, see the GTL Classroom Activity entitled Getting Ready for Life discussion related to the Choices We Make Matter—Now and in My Future.)

Below are GTL examples to use as you encourage and guide your middle and high school students to become self-managed on the first day of school, in the days that follow, and in their future.

---

**WHAT DO GREAT TEACHERS SAY WHEN…?**

**Encouraging Life-Long Self-Management (Classroom Behavior Standard 3.4)**

### GTL Reminders to Self:

*Remember*… Your goal this year is to help each student become self-managed. A self-managed student has made a conscious choice to demonstrate good behavior both in public and in private.

Words of Guidance

*Remember…* Remind your students every day of the importance of self-management, personal accountability, good behavior, and getting along with one another.
Words of Accountability

*Remember…* We encourage student self-management when we choose to persuade and help students adopt a pattern of good behavior over time, not when we coerce them or try to control them in the moment.
Words of Love

*Remember…* When we use our power and authority to coerce students into doing something, it might provide a short-term quick fix, but it doesn't persuade or empower students to become self-managed.
Words of Guidance

**GTL to Share with Students:**

"If you're not following our class rules and behavior expectations, I am going to talk with you about it, privately, and challenge you to think of specific things you can do to improve your behavior."
Words of Accountability

"You'll have lots of difficult choices to make this year. I want to help you understand that the choices you make matter, and I'll be here to help you with these decisions if you need me. Ultimately, you'll be making the decision and you'll be responsible for your choices."
Words of Guidance

"If I have a problem with you, I am going to quickly bring it to your attention, and if you have a problem with me or any other student, let us know as soon as possible. Let's address our concerns openly and honestly so we don't have any bad feelings for each other."
Words of Grace

"Every day, you'll have lots of choices to decide what you will say, what you will do, how you will act, and how you will treat others."

Words of Guidance

"My goal for each of you is that you will learn how to make the right choices both in school and outside of school."

Words of Guidance

"We're going to discuss important school policies you'll have to follow throughout the year and explain why they are important for everyone. We'll also talk about the consequences for not following each of the school policies."

Words of Accountability

"Based on our school policy discussion, now you know our school's policies, why they're important for everyone, and the consequences for not following them, and hopefully this information will help you make better choices throughout the year."

Words of Accountability

## Leading by Example

When teachers model appropriate language and actions, it gives clear direction to middle school and high school students. Modeling what you expect to hear and see from your students is the greatest way of leading by example and turning abstract concepts into concrete observable behaviors. Modeling an abstract concept like "respect" and discussing what it sounds like and looks like with your class helps students learn how to demonstrate respect for themselves and others. (See GTL Classroom Activity "Hit the Pause Button for Discussion on Student Behavior Expectations Related to Recognizing and Celebrating Mutual Respect in the Classroom When You See Multiple Students *Being*

*Respectful*" in Chapter 8.) During the first day of school and the days that follow, spend time discussing and role-playing with your students what difficult and ambiguous concepts sound like and look like. For example, encourage students to act out what grace and respect sound like and look like. Asking students for their input on how they would speak and act models for students your ability to respect their input and demonstrate grace when their responses need guidance. This culture of collaboration also models for students that "This is our school and our classroom. Let's agree on how we will talk to one another and treat each other."

It is important to model the behaviors you expect from your students and yourself every day. How are you going to model the behavior you hope to see? How will you model encouragement, grace, hope, love, and respect on the first day of school? We can miss the mark with students when we tell them to "show respect" without giving them specific examples of what respect looks like and sounds like. The following GTL examples illustrate what Words of Accountability, Words of Encouragement, Words of Grace, Words of Guidance, Words of High Expectations, Words of Hope, Words of Love, Words of Respect, Words of Relationship, Words of Understanding, and Words of Unity will look like and sound like in the classroom.

---

### WHAT DO GREAT TEACHERS SAY WHEN...?

**Leading by Example (Classroom Behavior Standard 3.5)**

### GTL Reminders to Self:

*Remember...* Think carefully about your Language of Practice, the tone of your voice, the words themselves, what you want to convey, the outcome you desire to see, and what you hope to inspire.

         Words of High Expectations

*Remember...* It is important to model hope for your students on the first day of school and the days that follow. When they see and hear you hoping for something and believing in something better, it gives them hope to do the same.

Words of Hope

*Remember…* When students see us modelling care for them, they are more likely to practice care for other students.

Words of Love

*Remember…* Model what you want your students to do. Be respectful, be on time, and be prepared.

Words of Accountability

*Remember…* On the first day of school, explain to your students that you are going to respect them and that you expect them to respect you.

Words of Respect

*Remember…* It's important to model and teach students how to respect each other and themselves by showing them what respect looks like and sounds like.

Words of Guidance

*Remember…* Grace is a powerful way to show patience and love for others.

Words of Grace

*Remember…* Asking students for their input about what respectful and disrespectful behaviors look like and sound like can help you better understand their perspective and their experiences.

Words of Understanding

**GTL to Share with Students:**

"Our words really do matter and make a difference. It's important for us to think about what we say to each other and how we say it."

Words of Unity

"Some of you might be wondering what you're doing in this class or what you're going to learn in this class, so I want to explain what we're learning, why we're learning it, and why it's important."
Words of Encouragement

"So, I want you to feel free this year to ask me why what we're learning is important, and I'll take the time to explain it."
Words of Relationship

"In our class, we are going to practice grace—and grace is offering others something they might not deserve."
Words of Grace

"I am going to try my best to model grace for you. Grace is offering others another chance to get things right. At some point, you might make a mistake—and I'll practice grace and offer you the support you need to do it better the next time."
Words of Grace

"I know I am not perfect and I'm going to make mistakes this year and when I do, I will be the first to apologize."
Words of Grace

"I want all of you to know I will be prepared for class every day, and I expect all of you to be prepared, too."
Words of High Expectations

"I want you all to know I won't expect anything of you I don't expect from myself. I will make sure I am in class on time, and I will follow our class rules and behavior expectations."
Words of High Expectations

"I am so excited to get to know each of you this year, and I want you to get to know me, so let me tell you something about myself."

Words of Relationship

"I plan to try to make everything we do relevant to you and to your life outside this classroom. What we say and do together will help you now and in your future."

Words of Encouragement

## Building Relationships with Students and Their Families

In your classroom, relationships are everything! We believe a Great Classroom Culture starts with a genuine care for middle school and high school students and their families. No matter what grade a student is in, all students need a teacher who cares about them, looks out for them, and guides them in love all along the way. This love is never to be confused with a 'romantic love' nor should this love be without accountability. Instead, this love is a caring and supporting love *with* accountability—the foundation for a strong relationship.

Teaching is a matter of the heart. The relationships you begin to develop with your students and their families on the first day and continue to strengthen throughout the year set the stage for deep trust and understanding. When teachers intentionally make an effort to connect with each student individually, it tells the student, "You are important to me" and "I care about you." In addition, when teachers intentionally make an effort to connect with the student's family, it shows the student and their family, "Your family is important to me" and "I care about your family." We believe getting to know middle school and high school students personally is a key to reaching them educationally. We also believe a strong relationship with the student's family significantly impacts their overall success in school. The following GTL examples and the GTL introductory parent phone call example below demonstrate an intentional desire to connect with students' and parents' hearts to build meaningful relationships.

---

**WHAT DO GREAT TEACHERS SAY WHEN…?**

**Building Relationships with Students and Their Families (Classroom Behavior Standard 3.6)**

**GTL Reminders to Self:**

*Remember…* Middle school and high school students need a teacher who wants the best for them and who is looking out for them and is working to develop relationships with them and their families.

Words of Relationship

*Remember…* Teaching is a matter of the heart.

Words of Love

*Remember…* It's important for your classroom to be ready and welcoming on the first day of school, but it's your commitment to care for and connect with your students and their families that will make the biggest difference.

Words of Love

*Remember…* Strong relationships with students and their families impact the overall success of students in school.

Words of Relationship

*Remember…* Every student is unique, and it's important for you to get to know each student individually.

Words of Understanding

*Remember…* Seize every opportunity to greet students with a smile, eye contact, and a kind word.

Words of Relationship

*Remember…* Look for opportunities to bond with your students. Walk with them in the hallways, talk with them about what's happening in their life, eat with them at lunch, support them in their sporting events and school activities, and laugh with them during class and after class.

Words of Relationship

*Remember…* When you call, email, or text parents about a student behavior issue concerning their child, be positive and respectful while sharing the truth about the situation.

Words of Respect

### GTL to Share with Students:

"I am here to help each one of you. Please don't hesitate to ask for help or to come to me for support."

Words of Love

"I am going to treat you the same way I want to be treated."

Words of Respect

"Hey, I noticed you shared a pencil with another student in our class today. I appreciate you doing that—it was very kind of you."

Words of Relationship

"You and your family are important to me, and I look forward to working with all of you this year."

Words of Love

"I'm excited to meet all of you today! This year we are going to be getting to know each other. I want to know what you're interested in, what you care about, and your favorite things to do."

Words of Relationship

"I am looking forward to getting to know your parents this year. I plan on staying connected with them so we can all help you be successful."

Words of Relationship

"We are all different and interesting in our own way. Some of us are outgoing and some of us are quiet. Let's try to get to know each other better this year. We can learn a lot from our differences."

Words of Understanding

**GTL to Use When Talking and Communicating with Parents:**

**Introductory phone call to the parents of your new students!**

(Note: This GTL phone conversation provides a template you can modify and send to parents as a letter, email, text message, etc.).

"Hello! My name is…. I'm excited to be Jamie's teacher this year! Is now a good time for us to talk?"

Words of Respect

"I wanted to reach out and introduce myself so you know more about me." (Share some personal and professional information that helps to build a relationship with the parent.)

Words of Relationship

"This year is going to be a great year for Jamie. There's so much to learn in (specific course), and I'm going to be here to help him and keep you informed all along the way."

Words of Hope

"As I'm getting to know Jamie this year, I'm going to talk to him about his strengths, hobbies, and interests—so I can encourage him and help him enjoy school and

get him thinking about setting goals for his future plans for high school, college and/or career, and life."
Words of High Expectations

"What are some of Jamie's strengths, hobbies, and interests?"
Words of Understanding

"I also want to share my contact information with you (share your school contact information) and let you know I'm available to answer any questions or concerns you have this year."
Words of Respect

"Today in class, we worked together to develop our rules and behavior expectations for our class and we created an agreement page for students, parents, and me to sign. Jamie will bring it home for you to sign and return to school. Our goal is understanding and agreement for everyone."
Words of Unity

"Maintaining a strong relationship and open communication between home and school is essential to Jamie's success this year."
Words of Relationship

"My goal is to keep you informed about what we are doing in my course, so you will know what to expect from me and what Jamie will be learning this year. On the school website, you will find our course portal. In that portal, you will find Jamie's weekly assignments and progress updates, along with his grades on assignments. You will have access to our course portal throughout the year. Please let me know if you have trouble accessing this information or if you have any questions about it."
Words of Guidance

> "Jamie and your family are important to me."
> Words of Love
>
> "I want to build a relationship with Jamie and your family this year. Our working together will help support his overall success in school."
> Words of Unity
>
> "If you can think of anything we can do to make things even better for Jamie this year, please let me know. My hope is for all our students to feel safe, enjoy school, learn as much as they can every day, and be ready for high school and life (use this with middle school students) or college and/or career and life (use this with high school students)."
> Words of Hope

## GTL Classroom Activities to Transform Middle School and High School Student Behavior and Your Classroom Culture

### GTL Classroom Activities for Middle School and High School Students on the First Day of School and the Days That Follow

We see these activities as either "in the moment" on the first day of school or a time to pull your students together for classroom conversations on the days that follow to encourage student voice and student engagement in your classroom. We see the teacher as a facilitator and co-learner during these GTL activities and students as active participants in learning how to "see the classroom through the lens of the teacher" and how to manage their own current behavior for success and their future behavior as they get ready for high school, college and/or a career.

1. (Role-play GTL Scenario Introduction on the First Day of School or on the Days that Follow.) Describe what a role-play is for the whole class. Tell them how you will pick different students or ask students to volunteer to participate in each role-play. Explain how the whole class will

be participating in specific role-plays to address certain issues that happen from time to time. Share with students how important role-playing is for practicing how to respectfully act and treat each other in the classroom. Also, share with students how role-playing will help them understand and demonstrate what positive behaviors will sound like and look like. In addition, explain to your students that role-playing will help them now and for their future. Start your first role-play activity. In this role-play, you (the teacher) will play yourself. This activity will allow you an opportunity to role-play how you will respectfully treat them (words and actions) when specific issues occur in your classroom. Select two students to role-play a specific issue, such as texting on their cell phones to one another during a class lesson, two students talking to one another while the teacher is trying to teach, or two students are arguing with each other. As the teacher, you will model for your students how to respectfully address the issue and remind the students of the rules and behavior expectations you all created together. Conclude the role-play by sharing with students that your respectful behavior (words and actions) is what they can expect from you as their teacher.

2. (Hit the Pause Button Introduction on the First Day of School or the Days that Follow for Setting up Teacher and Student Behavior Expectations, Classroom Rules, Group Work Norms and Discussing School Policies) Describe what a Hit the Pause Button discussion will look like for the whole class. Explain how you will "hit the pause button" to address certain issues that happen from time to time. Share with students how important learning is and how your Hit the Pause Button discussions are a quick way of addressing and resolving specific issues and getting everyone back to the lesson. Start your first Hit the Pause Button discussion. Describe how you and the students will collaborate to discuss and develop (a) a list of teacher and student behavior expectations for each other, (b) a list of your classroom rules for the year, and

(c) a list of group work norms for your class. In addition, discuss the school policies with them and allow them to ask questions and share their concerns. Explain how your teamwork approach is doing it "with them" and "not to them." The goal is to allow each student a chance to play an ownership role in the process and to share their thoughts and feelings on how everyone will act and treat each other in the class this year. Share with students the importance of agreeing on teacher and student behavior expectations, classroom rules, group work norms, and school policies and following them so every student feels safe, enjoys school, and learns as much as they can every day. As the teacher, you will have a tentative list of teacher and student behavior expectations, classroom rules, and your group work norms. You will also have a complete list of the school's policies to guide the discussion.

**Setting up Teacher and Student Behavior Expectations**
Start your discussion to determine "What You Can Expect from Me, As Your Teacher and What I Can Expect from You, As a Student". Pass around Post-it notes and ask your students to write down their expectations of you as their teacher and ask them to post their notes on a piece of poster paper in the class. Compile these responses into your list. Here is an example of a list of possible teacher behavior expectations based on GTL.

As your teacher,

- I will respect and care for you.
    (Words of Respect and Love)
- I will be prepared to teach you every day.
    (Words of Accountability)
- I will not embarrass you in front of the class.
    (Words of Grace and Relationship)
- I will be here to help you when you need me.
    (Words of Guidance and Hope)
- I will listen to you and encourage you.
    (Words of Understanding and Encouragement)

- I am going to challenge you to work hard and make good choices.
  (Words of High Expectations and Guidance)
- I am going to teach you new things this year, and I'll help you learn them.
  (Words of Accountability and Guidance)
- I am going to always be looking for win-win solutions for every situation.
  (Words of Encouragement and Hope)
- I am going to get to know you and connect with your parents this year.
  (Words of Relationship and Unity)

Then ask students to write down what the teacher can expect from them as a student on their Post-it notes. Ask the students to post their notes on the poster paper in the class. Spend some time discussing the student behavior expectations Post-it notes together. Compile these responses into your list.

The student behavior expectation list for the students could include the following:

As a student,

- I will respect the teacher and other students.
- I will be prepared and try hard to learn something new every day.
- I will work to get along with everyone.
- I will not embarrass other students or my teacher.
- I will make good choices.
- I will focus on learning.
- I will pay attention during lessons.
- I will avoid distractions.
- If I need help, I'll ask for help.
- I will work for win-win solutions with the teacher and other students.

After you've discussed the behavior expectations for everyone, explain to students how your lists might grow throughout the year if new behavior expectations need to be added.

### Setting Up Your Classroom Rules

The next part of the discussion will be using these behavior expectation lists to create your classroom rules together. Guide your students through the discussion and help them create rules that are appropriate for everyone. Once your classroom rules are agreed on, post them in the classroom where everyone can see them.

### Setting Up Your Group Work Norms

Next, take time to discuss and develop group work norms together. Explain to students how they will be doing a lot of collaboration and group work in your class. Group work will help them learn how to work as a team to achieve a shared goal. Provide an initial list of the group work norms you expect to see and ask students for additional suggestions.

### School Policy Discussion

Then share your school policies and open a discussion about them with your students. Prepare for this school policy discussion by having your notes and explanation for why each school policy is important for maintaining an ideal learning environment and ensuring everyone's safety. Allow time for students to ask questions about the policies and share their concerns.

Conclude all of the discussions by thanking all the students for working together to create the teacher and student behavior expectations, classroom rules, and group work norms. Remind students how you will share these teacher and student behavior expectations, classroom rules, group work norms, and school policies with their parents in the Student/Teacher/Parent Agreement. Their parents will sign the agreement and return it to the school. (Note: Please refer to your school's handbook and follow your school's policy related to other student/teacher/parent agreements.)

Throughout the first days of school, you can Hit the Pause Button for other discussions to include the following:

- ♦ Hit the Pause Button discussion for "Student Behavior Expectations Related to Attendance, Tardiness, and Skipping Class" in Chapter 4.

- Hit the Pause Button discussion for "Student Behavior Expectations Related to Academic Integrity and the Proper Use of Online Sources to Support Their Learning" in Chapter 5.
- Hit the Pause Button discussion for "Student Behavior Expectations and Communicating with Parents to Build Trust and Support Student Learning" in Chapter 6.
- Hit the Pause Button discussion on "Student Behavior Expectations Related to Inappropriate Outbursts When Students Yell, 'Why Do We Have to Learn This?'" in Chapter 7.
- Hit the Pause Button discussion on "Student Behavior Expectations Related to Recognizing and Celebrating Mutual Respect in the Classroom When You See Multiple Students Being Respectful" in Chapter 8.
- Hit the Pause Button discussion on "Student Behavior Expectations Related to Respectfully Sharing Disagreements and Opinions with Others When You See Students Having Disrespectful Disagreements in the Classroom with You and Other Students" in Chapter 9.
- Hit the Pause Button discussion on "Student Behavior Expectations Related to Your School's Policies on Bullying, Cyberbullying, and Fighting and What to Do if You are Bullied and How to Prevent a Fight" in Chapter 10.

3. Getting Ready for Life Discussion Introduction on the First Day of School or in the Days that Follow) Describe what a Getting Ready for Life discussion is for the whole class. Explain how the whole class, from time to time, will be participating in Getting Ready for Life discussions related to how the Choices We Make Matter—Now and in My Future. Tell them how you will begin these discussions to address life situations that all of them are facing and will continue to face throughout their lives. Explain how the Getting Ready for Life discussions are a way for them to think about certain life situations and how to make the best possible choices for themselves when they happen. Start your first Getting Ready for Life

discussion. In this Getting Ready for Life discussion, you and your students will be discussing how the Choices We Make Matter—Now and in My Future. Ask students to think about some possible choices they could make this week that could set them up for success this year. Also, ask students to think about the other choices they could make this week that could negatively impact their success and make their school year more difficult. Allow time for students to share their possible choices and encourage all of them to consider how the choices they make this week will impact the success of their school year. Conclude the discussion by reminding students how their personal success stories and great choices throughout the year might help and encourage other students to overcome the same or similar challenges and make great choices, too.

# 4

# What Do Great Teachers Say When a Student Seems Apathetic, Passively Disengaged, or Disconnected from School?

What do you say when you notice a middle school or a high school student who seems apathetic, passively disengaged, or disconnected from school (e.g., chronically absent, skipping school, sleeping, daydreaming, putting their head on their desk, or looking frustrated). This chapter provides teacher-friendly charts with Great Teacher Language (GTL) Reminders to Self, GTL to Share with Students, GTL to Use When Talking and Communicating with Parents, and GTL Classroom Activities specifically related to the following:

Scenario 4.1: A Student is Chronically Absent from School.
Scenario 4.2: A Student is Consistently Tardy to School or to a Particular Class.
Scenario 4.3: A Student is Skipping School All Day or Skipping a Particular Class During the Day.
Scenario 4.4: A Student is Sleeping During Class.
Scenario 4.5: A Student is Not Working on His Assignment and Looks Confused, Stressed, Or Frustrated.

**Scenario 4.6**: A Student Is Not Paying Attention to the Lesson, Is Uninterested, or Seems to Be Daydreaming In Class.
**Scenario 4.7**: A Student Never Verbally Participates In Class.
**Scenario 4.8**: A Passively Disengaged Student Has Failing Grades In Your Class.

> We know these are not the only apathetic, disconnected, or passively disengaged student behaviors that happen in your classroom. These specific scenarios are a starting point for you to develop your GTL for your classroom. For some of our student behavior scenarios, we have included GTL examples for you to use when talking with parents. These GTL examples are templates for phone conversations, emails, or other types of messages to develop strong communication between teachers and parents and to promote understanding, relationships, trust, and collaboration.

Apathetic, disconnected, or passively disengaged middle school or high school students present an interesting dilemma. While their behavior is usually not a disruption to others or the lesson, it is not acceptable behavior for the classroom. There is a tendency to ignore these students because they are not bothering anyone. However, their behavior is communicating something to us, and they need our help and guidance. When teachers address these passive behaviors to meet the individual student's needs, it not only helps the apathetic, disconnected, or passively disengaged student it also prevents the rest of the classroom from assuming that the behaviors are acceptable. Your Language of Practice (LoP) in the form of GTL can offer these passively disengaged students the accountability, encouragement, grace, guidance, high expectations, hope, love, relationships, respect, understanding, and unity necessary to successfully engage them in the learning.

Telling passively disengaged students to stop a certain behavior addresses the problem for the moment, but it is important to get to the root of the problem as well. Your words can help many passively disengaged students see the relevance and importance of staying engaged, interested, and involved so they can choose to behave appropriately. Your language can also help other students, with more personal issues, get the additional counselling and support they need. Your LoP in the form of GTL should demonstrate to students that what you teach is relevant, you expect their involvement, and you want to help them stay engaged in learning.

When middle school or high school students are disengaged, there is a tendency for us to react in a way to preserve our pride, dignity, and control. There is a big difference between a teacher exclaiming "You don't need to be sleeping in my class!" as opposed to pulling the student aside privately and asking "Is everything OK—I noticed that you were sleeping in class?" We believe it's important to respectfully understand the student's needs and their perspective. Why are they sleeping in class? Why are they skipping school? Why are they chronically absent? By separating the student from their behavior, we start to get a different picture of the circumstances surrounding the student's behavior. That's not to say that their behavior will be accepted in the classroom. However, when we have insight into why students are making certain choices, we get closer to understanding how to help them make better choices.

Many middle school and high school students don't see the value in school today, nor the value of an education for a lifetime. So many other fun and exciting technological distractions are much more interesting to them. It's no wonder that students are saying—or thinking to themselves—"School is sooooo boring!" These distractions make the passively disengaged students more difficult to reach. There is a whole world of real and virtual experiences that make schools appear less exciting and enjoyable. How can schools compete with that?

Often teachers feel the pressure to engage students by making everything fun and entertaining. Lights, camera, action, fun! But when the fun ends, the students tune out. Other teachers plan lessons that attempt to meet all students' interests, but is that possible all the time? The one thing teachers can do is to make their content relevant to all students. When teachers connect "the student's world" to the "world at large," the classroom lessons become more relevant, meaningful, helpful, valuable, and important to the students. This approach enables the passively disengaged students in your classroom to see "why they need to learn this information" and "how it's going to help them today and in the future."

Many passively disengaged middle school and high school students view school as an institution that forces them to do work rather than a place they enjoy where they can learn and grow and prepare for their future. School to them is unsatisfactory—boring and uninteresting. Is it important for students to enjoy school? Yes, it is. Enjoy means "with joy," and we define joy as a feeling of happiness or satisfaction that offers both immediate and long-term gratification. We believe there is a difference between the fun that students have outside of school or while on their phone gaming or watching videos—that ends when they enter the classroom or put their phone away—and the joy that students feel as they learn and work to reach their potential in school. When students experience the joy of learning for themselves, they understand the purpose of learning and the value of their education now and for their future. Our goal is to help passively disengaged students understand that learning can result in feelings of fun, satisfaction, and success. Your words can spark a student's interest and lead to student enjoyment and engagement in learning.

Many middle school and high school students who seem apathetic, disconnected, or passively disengaged fall through the cracks, give up, and eventually drop out of school. Often these students are not causing any trouble, so their behaviors are not classified as detrimental to the overall classroom environment. However, they hurt themselves, and their passive behaviors can lead to lifelong negative consequences. Day after day, these students may be unaware of the potential they have and the talents they possess. Teachers can make all the difference by helping passively disengaged students see how the day-to-day learning can spark their interests, explore their talents, and help them reach their potential and find success in school and in their future.

# WHAT DO GREAT TEACHERS SAY WHEN...?

**A Student is Chronically Absent from School. (Scenario 4.1)**

### GTL Reminders to Self:

*Remember...* We don't always know the whole story about what's going on with a student. Students who are chronically absent need your patience and your grace as they get the support they need to maintain regular attendance and participation in class.

Words of Grace

*Remember...* As you are caring for the chronically absent student, it will be important to connect with other school support team members (e.g., administrators, guidance counselors, or social workers) to get a better understanding of the needs of the student and their family.

Words of Understanding

*Remember...* Take every opportunity to have one-on-one conversations with your chronically absent students.

Words of Love

*Remember...* Sometimes students are chronically absent because of long-term physical problems. Be sure to be mindful of your students' physical needs as well as their learning needs.

Words of Understanding

*Remember...* Sometimes students are chronically absent because they struggle academically, they feel like school is too hard for them, or they have something going on at home.

Words of Understanding

*Remember...* Sometimes middle school and high school students who are chronically absent could have

part-time jobs to help support their families and might need your help with organizing their schedule.
Words of Respect

*Remember…* Middle school and high school students might be responsible for other siblings or family members at home and miss school to meet that responsibility. Talk with your chronically absent student to offer your help and support.
Words of Guidance

**GTL to Share with Students:**

(Whispering to student) "I am worried about you being absent from school. Can you tell me what's going on?"
Words of Understanding

"I'm concerned about the way you've been absent from school. Is everything OK?"
Words of Love

"When you miss class for an absence, I can send your missed work home to you. Don't forget to let me know when I can do that for you. I don't want you to get behind in your work because you have been absent."
Words of Grace

"Let's discuss the school's policy about attendance and why we have this policy." (Discuss your school's attendance policy with the whole class.)
Words of Accountability

"Is there anything at all I can do to help you so that you can get to school more consistently?"
Words of Understanding

(Proactive one-on-one conversation with a student who has recently been absent several days to check on them and remind them of your school's attendance policy) "I've noticed you've been absent a lot recently, and I want to work with you and your family to make sure you don't miss more days than the attendance policy allows."

Words of Accountability

"Let's set up a meeting with you, your parents, and the guidance counselor to talk about how we can support you and your family, so you can take care of your needs at home and be successful in school."

Words of Guidance

"Our school has a lot of resources to support you and your family if you need them. I can help connect you and your family to them."

Words of Unity

"You might have an unforeseen issue that causes you to be absent. Please let me know if I can help you with anything, and I'll work with you."

Words of Grace

"You might be feeling behind because of your absences, but I'm going to work with you so you get caught up with your work and you can begin to feel confident in yourself."

Words of Hope

**GTL to Use When Talking and Communicating with Parents:**

**Phone call to parent to show concern about their child who has been chronically absent from school.**

(Note: This GTL phone conversation provides a template you can modify and send to parents as a letter, email, text message, etc.).

"Hello! My name is…. I'm Jamie's teacher. He's not in trouble. Is now a good time for us to talk?"
Words of Respect

"I enjoy having Jamie in my class. He is…(share something personal, positive, and specific that you've experienced with Jamie and link it to a positive quality that could help Jamie in his future in high school, college or career, and life."
Words of Encouragement

"I'm calling you because I've noticed that Jamie has been absent several days recently, and I wanted to check to see if everything is OK with him and your family."
Words of Accountability

"I wanted to mention this to you and work with you and Jamie on a plan for helping him make up the work he has missed."
Words of Grace

"I also want you to know our school has a lot of resources that can support Jamie and your family if there's anything you need. I can help connect you and your family to them."
Words of Love

"Please let me know if you have any questions at all. My hope is for all our students to feel safe, enjoy school, learn as much as they can every day, and be ready for high school and life (use this with middle school students) or college or career and life (use this with high school students)."
Words of Hope

## WHAT DO GREAT TEACHERS SAY WHEN...?

**A Student is Consistently Tardy to School or to a Particular Class. (Scenario 4.2)**

### GTL Reminders to Self:

*Remember…* We don't always know the whole story about what's going on with a student. Students who are consistently tardy to school may have transportation issues they cannot control.

Words of Understanding

*Remember…* Take every opportunity to have one-on-one conversations with your consistently tardy students. Try to find out the reasons they might be arriving late for school or the reasons they are late getting to your class.

Words of Love

*Remember…* Sometimes students are consistently tardy to your class because they struggle academically with the content in your class or they feel like school is too hard for them.

Words of Understanding

*Remember…* Middle school and high school students might be responsible for other siblings or family members at home and arrive at school late because of that responsibility. Talk with the consistently tardy student to offer your help and support.

Words of Guidance

*Remember…* Most middle school and high school students enjoy socializing before and after class in the hallways. Sometimes this results in their being late to your class. Consider providing time during your class for students to socialize with one another.

Words of Relationship

*Remember...* Encourage your students to be on time for class and remind them that tardiness creates distractions for the whole class, so they need to enter the room quietly and respectfully.
Words of Accountability

*Remember...* Unforeseen things or possibly embarrassing things may cause students to be tardy.
Words of Grace

**GTL to Share with Students:**

(Whispering to student) "I am concerned about you being tardy to my class each day. Can you tell me what's going on?"
Words of Understanding

"I'm concerned about the way you've been tardy to school. Is everything OK?"
Words of Love

(Shared privately to help a consistently tardy student feel connected to your class) "I was wondering if you would be interested in helping me lead a discussion tomorrow in class. I'll provide the questions you will ask the other students."
Words of Relationship

(Shared with the whole class) "Let's have a class conversation about being tardy to class. What are some of the reasons you might be late for class? What are some suggestions for avoiding being late for class?"
Words of Unity

"Let's discuss the school's policy about tardiness and why we have this policy." (Discuss your school's tardy policy with the whole class.)
Words of Accountability

"Tardiness creates distractions for the whole class. So if you are tardy for class, please enter our classroom quietly and respectfully."
Words of Respect

"Is there anything at all I can do to help you get to class on time?"
Words of Understanding

"You might have an unforeseen issue that causes you to be tardy for class. Please let me know if I can help you with anything, and I'll work with you."
Words of Grace

"If you are consistently tardy for school because you have a transportation issue, please let me know."
Words of Understanding

**GTL to Use When Talking and Communicating with Parents:**

**Phone call to parent to show concern about their child, who has been chronically tardy from school.**

(Note: This GTL phone conversation provides a template you can modify and send to parents as a letter, email, text message, etc.).

"Hello! My name is…. I'm Jamie's teacher. He's not in trouble. Is now a good time for us to talk?"
Words of Respect

"I enjoy having Jamie in my class. He is… (share something personal, positive, and specific that you've experienced with Jamie and link it to a positive quality that could help Jamie in his future in high school, college or career, and life)."
Words of Encouragement

"I'm calling you because I've noticed that Jamie has been tardy to school and my class several days recently, and I wanted to check to see if everything is OK with him and your family."

Words of Accountability

"I wanted to mention this to you and work with you and Jamie on a plan for helping him get to school and my class on time."

Words of Grace

"I also want you to know that, for all of our students, our school offers transportation that can serve Jamie and your family. I can help connect you and your family to someone who can help you with this transportation service."

Words of Love

"Please let me know if you have any questions at all. My hope is for all our students to feel safe, enjoy school, learn as much as they can every day, and be ready for high school and life (use this with middle school students) or college or career and life (use this with high school students)."

Words of Hope

## WHAT DO GREAT TEACHERS SAY WHEN…?

**A Student is Skipping School All Day or Skipping a Particular Class During the Day. (Scenario 4.3)**

### GTL Reminders to Self:

*Remember…* We don't always know the whole story about what's going on with a student. Students who are skipping school or your class need your patience, your understanding, and your grace as you dig deeper to discover the reasons they are skipping school or your class.

Words of Grace

*Remember…* Take every opportunity to have one-on-one conversations with a student who is choosing to skip school or your class. Talking and connecting with these students will help to develop a relationship with them and hopefully impact their decision to attend school or your class.

Words of Relationship

*Remember…* Sometimes students skip your class because they don't see the need to attend, they don't understand the relevance of the class, or they are not interested in learning the content.

Words of Understanding

*Remember…* Sometimes students skip school or your class because they struggle academically, they feel like school is too hard for them, or they have something going on at home or in their life.

Words of Understanding

*Remember…* Sometimes middle school and high school students who skip school have part-time jobs to help support their families and might need your help organizing their schedules and learning how to manage both responsibilities.

Words of Respect

*Remember…* Middle school and high school students might be responsible for other siblings or family members at home and miss school to meet that responsibility. Talk with your student who skips school or your class to offer your help and support.

Words of Guidance

*Remember…* Sometimes students might skip school or your class because they don't have great relationships with their peers or they're afraid of other students.
Words of Understanding

*Remember…* Sometimes students might skip school or your class because they are peer-pressured into doing it.
Words of Relationship

*Remember…* Unforeseen things or possibly embarrassing things may cause students to skip school or your class.
Words of Grace

**GTL to Share with Students:**

(Whispering to student) "I am concerned about you skipping my class. Can you tell me what's going on?"
Words of Understanding

"I'm concerned about the way you've been skipping my class. Is everything OK?"
Words of Love

(Shared privately to help a student who has been skipping your class feel connected to your class) "I was wondering if you would be interested in helping me lead a discussion tomorrow in class. I'll provide the questions you will ask the other students."
Words of Relationship

(Shared with the whole class) "Let's have a class conversation about skipping school and skipping class. What are some of the reasons you might be skipping class? What are some short-term and long-term consequences of skipping class?"
Words of Unity

"Let's discuss the school's policy about skipping school and skipping class and why we have this policy." (With the whole class, discuss your school's policy for skipping school and skipping class.)
Words of Accountability

(Private conversation with student who is skipping school and your class) "I've been missing you in my class. Is there any way I can help you get started with the work you have missed?"
Words of Grace

"I respect you and want you to be successful in my class. For you to be successful in my class, you're going to need to make the important choice to attend and participate in class so you can enjoy success during school and then enjoy your free time after school."
Words of Respect

"Is there anything at all I can do to encourage you to attend school and my class?"
Words of Encouragement

"You might have an unforeseen issue that causes you to skip school or skip class. Please let me know if I can help you with anything, and I'll work with you."
Words of Grace

"If you are skipping school or class because you have a transportation issue, please let me know."
Words of Understanding

**GTL to Use When Talking and Communicating with Parents:**

**Phone call to parent to show concern about their child who has been skipping your class.**

(Note: This GTL phone conversation provides a template you can modify and send to parents as a letter, email, text message, etc.).

"Hello, my name is.... I'm Jamie's teacher. He's not in trouble. Is now a good time for us to talk?"
Words of Respect

"I enjoy having Jamie in my class. He is… (share something personal, positive, and specific that you've experienced with Jamie and link it to a positive quality that could help Jamie in his future in high school, college or career, and life)."
Words of Encouragement

"I'm calling you because I've noticed that Jamie has skipped my class several days recently, and I wanted to check to see if everything is OK with him and your family."
Words of Accountability

"I spoke with Jamie today and told him I respect him and want him to be successful in my class. I also told him that in order for him to be successful in my class, he's going to need to make the important choice to attend and participate in class so he can enjoy success during school and then enjoy his free time after school."
Words of Relationship

"I wanted to mention this to you and work with you and Jamie on a plan for helping him get to school and my class each day."
Words of Grace

"I also want you to know that, for all of our students, our school offers transportation that can serve Jamie and your family. I can help connect you and your family to someone who can help you with this transportation service."
Words of Love

"Please let me know if you have any questions at all. My hope is for all our students to feel safe, enjoy school, learn as much as they can every day, and be ready for high school and life (use this with middle school students) or college or career and life (use this with high school students)."

Words of Hope

## WHAT DO GREAT TEACHERS SAY WHEN…?

**A Student is Sleeping During Class. (Scenario 4.4)**

### GTL Reminders to Self:

*Remember…* Take care of the things you can change and be mindful and aware of the things you cannot change.

Words of Grace

*Remember…* We don't always know the whole story about what's going on with a student. Students who are sleeping in your class need your patience, your understanding, and your grace as you dig deeper to discover the reasons they are sleeping in your class.

Words of Grace

*Remember…* Take every opportunity to have one-on-one conversations with a student who is sleeping in your class. Talking and connecting with these students will help to develop a relationship with them and hopefully impact their decision to stay awake and engage in your class.

Words of Relationship

*Remember…* Sometimes students sleep in class because they're tired, they don't see the need to pay attention,

they don't understand the relevance of the class, or they are not interested in learning the content.
Words of Understanding

*Remember...* Sometimes students sleep in your class because they struggle academically, they feel like school is too hard for them, or they have something going on at home or in their life.
Words of Understanding

*Remember...* Sometimes middle school and high school students who sleep in your class have part-time jobs to help support their families and might need your help organizing their schedules and learning how to manage both responsibilities, so they can get the sleep they need.
Words of Respect

*Remember...* Middle school and high school students might be responsible for other siblings or family members at home. Talk with your student who sleeps in class to offer your help and support.
Words of Guidance

*Remember...* Sometimes students might pretend to sleep in your class because they don't have great relationships with their peers or they're afraid of other students.
Words of Understanding

*Remember...* Unforeseen things or possibly embarrassing things may cause students to sleep in your class.
Words of Grace

### GTL to Share with Students:

(Whispering to student) "I am concerned about you sleeping in my class. Can you tell me what's going on?"
Words of Understanding

"I'm concerned about the way you've been sleeping in my class. Is everything OK?"

Words of Love

"I understand that you are feeling sleepy. That must be a difficult way to feel at school. How can I help you? Do you want to talk? Is there anything I can do to help?"

Words of Understanding

(Shared privately to help a student who has been sleeping in your class feel connected to your class) "I was wondering if you would be interested in helping me lead a discussion tomorrow in class. I'll provide the questions you will ask the other students."

Words of Relationship

(Shared with the whole class) "Let's have a class conversation about sleeping in class. What are some of the reasons you might be sleeping in class? What are some short-term and long-term consequences of sleeping in class?"

Words of Unity

"Let's discuss the school's policy related to sleeping in class and why we have this policy." (With the whole class, discuss your school's policy related to sleeping in class.)

Words of Accountability

"Let's talk about your schedule and the things that are keeping you from getting the sleep you need so you can be awake during the school day."

Words of Accountability

"I respect you and want you to be successful in my class. For you to be successful in my class, you're going to need to make the important choice to stay awake and participate in class so you can enjoy success during school and then enjoy your free time and sleep after school.

Words of Respect

"Is there anything at all I can do to encourage you to stay awake in my class?"

Words of Encouragement

"You might have an issue that causes you to sleep in class. Please let me know if I can help you with anything, and I'll work with you."

Words of Grace

**GTL to Use When Talking and Communicating with Parents:**

**Phone call to parent to let them know their child has been sleeping in class.**

(Note: This GTL phone conversation provides a template you can modify and send to parents as a letter, email, text message, etc.).

"Hello! My name is…. I'm Jamie's teacher. He's not in trouble. Is now a good time for us to talk?"

Words of Respect

"I enjoy having Jamie in my class. He is… (share something personal, positive, and specific that you've experienced with Jamie and link it to a positive quality that could help Jamie in his future in high school, college or career, and life)."

Words of Encouragement

"I'm calling you to share something that happened today at school. Jamie seemed extremely tired today. He slept during class."

Words of Accountability

"I spoke with Jamie in private to find out if he was feeling OK. I wanted to make sure he wasn't sick or needed to go see the school nurse or call home."

Words of Love

"I wanted to mention this to you and work with you on a plan for addressing this sleeping issue, so Jamie can experience success in our class."

Words of Unity

"Please let me know if you have any questions at all. My hope is for all our students to feel safe, enjoy school, learn as much as they can every day, and be ready for high school and life (use this with middle school students) or college or career and life (use this with high school students)."

Words of Hope

## WHAT DO GREAT TEACHERS SAY WHEN…?

**A Student is Not Working on His Assignment and Looks Confused, Stressed, Or Frustrated. (Scenario 4.5)**

### GTL Reminders to Self:

*Remember…* When you separate the student from his/her behavior—in this case, the student who is not working on his assignment in class—it allows you to 'take a step back' and let the student know "I still care for you, but I don't like the choice you are making right now."

Words of Grace

*Remember…* When you show that you care, students who look confused, stressed, or frustrated will respond.

Words of Relationship

*Remember*... Be on the lookout for potential moments when students might feel confused or frustrated. Confusion and frustration can lead to shame, self-consciousness, and disengagement with the lesson.
Words of Guidance

*Remember*... Middle school and high school students might not be willing to share with you that they are confused about their work, especially in front of their peers.
Words of Understanding

*Remember*... When students are stressed or frustrated about the assignment or the project in your class, they often just shut down and stop trying.
Words of Understanding

*Remember*... When you respectfully reach out to confused, stressed, or frustrated students, you are offering them the support they need to be successful in your class.
Words of Respect

### GTL to Share with Students:

(Whispering to student) "It's not fair to the other students—or to you—if you are not working on the assignment that we're all working on."
Words of Accountability

"I am sorry—I didn't realize you were confused and weren't able to complete the assignment. Sometimes it may take me a while to understand what you are saying or what you need."
Words of Grace

"I noticed you looked stressed. How can I help you?"
Words of Love

"You look frustrated. Let's talk about what's frustrating you today, and we can decide how to work through this problem together so it won't frustrate you tomorrow."

Words of Hope

"Whenever learning becomes difficult for you, don't allow yourself to feel stupid or frustrated, because then you might become discouraged and give up. I'm going to help you avoid those feelings by answering all of your questions and teaching you how to learn new information."

Words of Encouragement

"How can I help you finish this assignment?"

Words of Relationship

"I respect you and want you to be successful in my class. For you to be successful in my class, you're going to need to make the important choice to ask for help when you're confused, stressed, or frustrated. My hope is for you to finish this assignment so you can enjoy success during school."

Words of Respect

## WHAT DO GREAT TEACHERS SAY WHEN…?

**A Student Is Not Paying Attention to the Lesson, Is Uninterested, or Seems to Be Daydreaming In Class. (Scenario 4.6)**

### GTL Reminders to Self:

*Remember…* Whenever it is possible, try to get to know your students. Talk to them and get to know what they like or dislike. Try to find out what their passions are and what they really care about.

Words of Relationship

*Remember…* Students' perceptions guide their feelings, and to truly understand their feelings, it's important to acknowledge those perceptions.

Words of Understanding

*Remember…* Sometimes students don't pay attention and daydream because they don't understand the lesson, they have something going on at home, or they're bored.

Words of Understanding

*Remember…* Middle school and high school students might be thinking about their plans after school. This could give you an opportunity to make a connection with them.

Words of Relationship

*Remember…* Middle school and high school students are learning how to manage their own personal lives and independence but will still need guidance to balance school, home, and friendships.

Words of Guidance

Remember… It's important for our lessons to be engaging and relevant for our students and for us to explain why they need to learn it.

Words of Accountability

**GTL to Share with Students:**

"It seems like you have something on your mind. Do you want to talk about it? I want to help you get to a point where you can focus on your work.

Words of Relationship

"You don't seem like yourself today. I have noticed you are having trouble paying attention and might need my help. Let's talk after class."

Words of Love

"When you're starting to get confused and tune out from our lesson, just ask me for help."
Words of Guidance

(Shared privately to help a student who seems uninterested or is daydreaming in your class feel connected to your class) "I was wondering if you would be interested in helping me lead a discussion tomorrow in class. I'll provide the questions you will ask the other students."
Words of Relationship

(Whispering to student) "I know this assignment is confusing right now, but remember it's so important to pay attention to our lesson. When it clicks for you and you finally understand how to do it, you'll feel good about it."
Words of Encouragement

(To the whole class) "My goal is to make every lesson engaging and relevant. So you can see why it's important to learn now and for your future."
Words of Hope

"You seem uninterested in the lesson today. How can I help you? Do you want to talk? Is there anything I can do to help?"
Words of Understanding

## WHAT DO GREAT TEACHERS SAY WHEN…?

**A Student Never Verbally Participates In Class. (Scenario 4.7)**

### GTL Reminders to Self:

*Remember…* Passively disengaged students often blend in and choose not to participate. See them as potential contributors and encourage them to be an active participant in your classroom.
Words of Hope

*Remember...* A classroom filled with hope brings energy to the students and the teacher.
Words of Hope

*Remember...* Sometimes students don't participate, because they're shy, introverted, or afraid to speak out.
Words of Understanding

*Remember...* Sometimes students don't participate, because they are slow readers or they have a speech impairment. This awareness could be an opportunity to connect these students with the special services they need to be successful.
Words of Understanding

*Remember...* A student who never verbally participates in class and seems to be apathetic might be afraid they may be wrong when answering a question and people might laugh at them.
Words of Understanding

*Remember...* A passively disengaged student might have personal issues that are preventing them from verbally engaging in the lesson.
Words of Relationship

*Remember...* A student who never verbally participates in class and appears to be disconnected from school might have a conflict with another student in your class and doesn't want to talk in class.
Words of Understanding

### GTL to Share with Students:

(To the whole class) "I know you might be afraid to speak out in class, but I promise we want to hear what you have to say, what you believe, and the questions you have."
Words of Encouragement

"I understand if you don't feel like talking about it right now—just know I'm available to listen when you feel like it."

Words of Understanding

(To the whole class) "This lesson is going to be great! It's going to be relevant and something we all need to know, so I'll be expecting everyone's participation."

Words of High Expectations

"I can see you one day running your own business, being a fireman, teaching students in your own classroom, being a nurse in a hospital, or whatever you hope to be."

Words of Hope

"I care about you and want you to be successful. Help me understand what I can do to help you get involved in our classroom discussions."

Words of Understanding

(To the whole class) "In our class, we want to establish a climate where no one feels embarrassed to share. We will work together to respect each other's opinions and thoughts."

Words of Respect

"Don't be afraid to share your thoughts with the class during our class discussion. We want to hear what you have to say. I know you can do this."

Words of High Expectations

"I understand you are hesitant to be the leader for your group. But I know you can do it because you have the qualities of a good leader. You're a good listener and you treat everybody with respect and dignity."

Words of Relationship

## WHAT DO GREAT TEACHERS SAY WHEN...?

**A Passively Disengaged Student Has Failing Grades In Your Class. (Scenario 4.8)**

### GTL Reminders to Self:

*Remember...* Sometimes students disengage because of a fear of failure.

Words of Understanding

*Remember...* Sometimes students have failing grades because they don't see how the lesson relates to them and their world and they stop trying.

Words of Relationship

*Remember...* Sometimes students have failing grades because they're shy, introverted, or afraid to speak out, causing them to slip through the cracks.

Words of Understanding

*Remember...* Sometimes students have failing grades because they are slow readers.

Words of Understanding

*Remember...* When students are disappointed about their failing grade on an assignment, encourage them not to give up. Consider helping them create a plan to redo the assignment.

Words of Encouragement

*Remember...* Students can have failing grades because of academic issues, social issues, behavior issues, homework issues, apathy issues, or lack of interest.

Words of Understanding

*Remember...* It's important to be proactive with students who are failing your class and reach out to their parents. The sooner you engage them in addressing the failing grades, the sooner the student will see your support and have a better chance of passing the course. (See Parent Phone call template below.)

Words of Guidance

### GTL to Share with Students:

"I want to help you in any way possible—I'll spend extra time with you to work on this class."

Words of Guidance

(Whispering to student) "You've almost got it. I know this is challenging, but when you finish this project, you'll feel great!"

Words of Encouragement

"I am excited to see you are enjoying our group activity today and working hard to complete your part of it. I knew you could do it!"

Words of High Expectations

"Let's look at how this lesson is impacting your world today and how it relates to you, your family, and your community."

Words of Relationship

"I can tell you're really disappointed about your test grade and you might want to give up. Let's make a plan together so you can succeed next time."

Words of Encouragement

"It looks like you need a chance to redo this assignment. I know you can do better than this, and I want to help you get there."

Words of Grace

"Don't keep being hard on yourself about your past grades. Let's put those behind us and move ahead!"

Words of Grace

"When you have tried your very best at something and it still doesn't seem good enough, don't give up and stop trying. We'll keep working together to figure it out."

Words of Unity

"I know you are still struggling with the work in this class, but every day you are working harder and harder and you are improving. You're doing exactly what you need to do to be successful in high school, college or career, and life."

Words of Encouragement

**GTL to Use When Talking and Communicating with Parents:**

**Phone call to parent to discuss child's failing grades, share our concerns, and work together to create a support plan for their child both at school and at home.**

(Note: This GTL phone conversation provides a template you can modify and send to parents as a letter, email, text message, etc.).

"Hello! My name is…. I'm Jamie's teacher. He's not in trouble. Is now a good time for us to talk?"

Words of Respect

"I enjoy having Jamie in my class. He is… (share something personal, positive, and specific that you've experienced with Jamie and link it to a positive quality that could help Jamie in his future in high school, college or career, and life)."

Words of Encouragement

"I wanted to call and share an update on how Jamie is doing in class."

Words of Relationship

"Jamie is having trouble with some of the work we're doing, and I'm concerned about him and his grades right now. If you remember, you and I talked at our Open House about how all of Jamie's weekly assignments, progress updates, and assignment grades would be posted on our course portal on the school website. I would like to discuss Jamie's progress with you and a plan to support him."

Words of Accountability

"I've been talking to Jamie and working with him individually, and I also need your insight and influence and help. Could we meet sometime this week and sit down together to design the support plan for Jamie? Together, we can get him the support he needs to be successful."

Words of Unity

"When would be a good time for you to meet?"

Words of Respect

"I'm looking forward to meeting with you and working together for Jamie. He has plenty of time to catch up and get back on track."

Words of Hope

"Please let me know if you have any questions at all. My hope is for all our students to feel safe, enjoy school, learn as much as they can every day, and be ready for high school and life (use this with middle school students) or college or career and life (use this with high school students)."

Words of Hope

## GTL Classroom Activities to Transform Middle School and High School Student Behavior and Your Classroom Culture

### GTL Classroom Activities for Students Who Seem Apathetic, Passively Disengaged, or Disconnected from Middle School and High School

We see these activities as either "in the moment" or a time to pull your students together for classroom conversations to encourage student voice and student engagement in your classroom.

We see the teacher as a facilitator and co-learner during these GTL activities and students as active participants in learning how to "see the classroom through the lens of the teacher" and how to manage their own current behavior for success and their future behavior as they get ready for high school, college or a career.

1. (Role-Play GTL Scenario for students who are passively not paying attention, including sleeping in class, daydreaming in class, uninterested in class, and skipping school) Select one student to role-play a teacher and one student to role-play a student who is passively not paying attention in class (e.g., sleeping in class, daydreaming in class, uninterested in class, or skipping school). Allow time for the role-playing teacher to try to engage the passively disengaged student. After the first role-play, ask the passively disengaged student who was sleeping in class if what the role-playing teacher said was helpful. Encourage the other students in the class to help the role-playing teacher with what to say and how to respectfully respond to the passively disengaged student who is sleeping in class, so they will start to pay attention and engage in class. Continue the role-play with the other passively disengaged student scenarios. Conclude each role-playing activity with a discussion of how you, as the teacher, will respectfully engage passively disengaged students in your classroom.

2. (Hit the Pause Button for Discussion on Student Behavior Expectations Related to Attendance, Tardiness, and Skipping Class.) Share with the students that you are

going to "Hit the Pause Button" on the lesson and take important time to discuss the school policies related to attendance, tardiness, and skipping class. Ask students to share the things that cause them to be absent, tardy, and skip school. Allow time for each student to share one of their things with the class. Discuss why these policies are important and how student attendance and participation in class will ensure their success now and for their future. Conclude the discussion by encouraging your students to reach out to you when unforeseen things happen that cause them to be absent, tardy, or skip school.

3. (Getting Ready for Life Discussion about Overcoming Distractions and Making Great Choices) Share with the students that you're about to have a Getting Ready for Life discussion related to overcoming distractions and making great choices. Explain to students how everyone faces challenges and how we all have to overcome distractions and make great choices to be successful in school and in life. Break the class into small discussion groups. First, ask students to think about some distractions they face in school every day. Then, ask the students to share their success stories—what they've done in the past to make great choices to avoid or eliminate their distractions. Finally, ask students to collaborate and come up with strategies they could use to avoid or eliminate distractions to set themselves up for success this year. Circulate around the classroom to listen in on the small group discussions. Allow time for students to share these distractions and their strategies for making great choices in their small group. Bring the whole class back together and ask if any group wants to share with the whole class. Remind students how their personal success stories might help and encourage another student to overcome the same or similar challenges with eliminating distractions. Conclude the discussion by sharing how making great choices and eliminating distractions today will set them up for success for high school, college or career, and life.

# 5

# What Do Great Teachers Say to Encourage Proper Use of Technology and Devices in the Classroom?

What do you say when you notice a student is off-task, texting on his/her phone, watching a video, listening to music, or searching online for personal reasons? This chapter provides teacher-friendly charts with Great Teacher Language (GTL) Reminders to Self, GTL to Share with Students, GTL to Use When Talking and Communicating with Parents, and GTL Classroom Activities specifically related to the following:

Scenario 5.1: A Student is Off-task and Texting on His/Her Phone.

Scenario 5.2: A Student is Off-task, Playing a Video Game, Watching a Video, or Watching a Movie on His Phone/Computer.

Scenario 5.3: A Student is Off-task and Listening to Music on His/Her Phone (Using Ear Buds).

Scenario 5.4: A Student is Off-task and Searching Online for Personal Reasons.

Scenario 5.5: A Student is Plagiarizing Other People's Work and/Or Copying Answers from Online Sources.

> We know these are not the only off-task student behaviors related to inappropriate technology use in your classroom. These specific scenarios are a starting point for you to develop your GTL for your classroom. For some of our student behavior scenarios, we have included GTL examples for you to use when talking with parents. These GTL examples are templates for phone conversations, emails, or other types of messages to develop strong communication between teachers and parents and to promote understanding, relationships, trust, and collaboration.

Today's middle school and high school students have an abundance of technological devices at their fingertips. These students have no recollection of a life or a world without these devices. They have all been living in a technologically advanced world where screen time and social media can dominate their time and their attention. Our students need our help and guidance to use these new technologies to enhance their learning and not derail it. Your Language of Practice (LoP) in the form of GTL can offer these students the accountability, encouragement, grace, guidance, high expectations, hope, love, relationships, respect, understanding, and unity necessary to successfully engage them in the learning.

It seems like for every advantage to using technology in schools, there's a resulting challenge that teachers face in the classroom. The advantages include quick access to unlimited information, helpful applications that support real-time and online collaboration, and enhanced multisensory learning, just to name a few. The resulting challenges include an overload of information that's almost impossible to filter through, real-time and online collaboration can turn into social conversations that get students off-task, and multisensory learning can lead to screen time all the time.

When teachers are able to carefully integrate this technology into a truly enhanced, real-time learning environment, the results can be great! However, the overwhelming magnetic pull of technology can distract every student and educator at some point each day. Our goal as educators is to integrate technology and maximize personalized and individualized learning for all students.

It is important for teachers to provide students and parents with clear expectations about the proper use of technology and devices in their classrooms. Teachers can make all the difference when they clearly explain to students and parents that while technology can be a helpful tool in the classroom for teaching and learning, it can also be a tool that distracts students from the real-time learning in the moment and negatively impacts their learning and success in school and in their future.

---

### WHAT DO GREAT TEACHERS SAY WHEN…?

**A Student is Off-task and Texting on His/Her Phone. (Scenario 5.1)**

#### GTL Reminders to Self:

*Remember…* Creating engaging and relevant lessons will help keep students tuned in to real-time learning instead of their personal screen time.

Words of Guidance

*Remember…* By proactively circulating around your classroom and paying attention to the needs of your students, you can prevent students from becoming distracted by technology devices.

Words of Understanding

*Remember…* There's a strong magnetic pull to devices.

Words of Relationship

*Remember…* Some students will choose to text on their phone during class and will disengage from the lesson, and they will need to be respectfully redirected back to the lesson.

Words of Grace

*Remember…* Technology is here to stay. It can be a helpful tool in the classroom for teaching and learning. It can also be a tool that distracts students from the real-time learning in the moment and negatively impacts their learning and success over time.

Words of Guidance

*Remember…* Be mindful that you need to demonstrate a balance of love and authority when it comes to technology. Too much love with no authority can lead to no boundaries for students and their personal devices. Too much authority with no love can create a "lose-lose" situation, for both the teacher and the student. In this "lose-lose" situation, the student could 'lose' the connection and relationship with their teacher, and the teacher could 'lose' the student's willingness to cooperate.

Words of Love

*Remember…* It's going to be important for you to have a whole class conversation about technology use and personal devices and make sure everyone understands the expectations about technology use in the classroom.

Words of Unity

*Remember…* It's important for students to hear that you want to respect their privacy and the personal use of their devices. So, explain to students the importance of respecting the class lesson time and agree that everyone, including you, will put their phones away during the lesson.

Words of Respect

*Remember…* Students may need their personal devices for emergencies.

Words of Relationship

**GTL to Share with Students:**

"I know you enjoy texting on your phone to your friends. I enjoy texting my friends, too."
Words of Relationship

"But this isn't the right time for that."
Words of Accountability

"I'm going to give you a minute to make the mental shift back to what we're doing."
Words of Guidance

"It looks like there's something important on your phone. Is everything OK?"
Words of Love

"Remember our class expectations about using phones during class? If it's an emergency, please let me know and you can use it. If it's not an emergency, please put it away so you can get back to our lesson."
Words of Respect

(Shared with the whole class) "I understand how technology has this magnetic pull and how you can easily get distracted with texting on your phone."
Words of Understanding

"Let's discuss the school's policy about proper cell phone use in the classroom and why we have this policy." (Discuss your school's cell phone use policy with the whole class.)
Words of Accountability

**GTL to Use When Talking and Communicating with Parents:**

Phone call to discuss appropriate cell phone use in the classroom: A student is consistently off-task and texting on his cell phone, which distracts him from the lesson.

(Note: This GTL phone conversation provides a template you can modify and send to parents as a letter, email, text message, etc.).

"Hello! My name is…. I'm Jamie's teacher. He's not in trouble. Is now a good time for us to talk?"
Words of Respect

"I enjoy having Jamie in my class. He is… (share something personal, positive, and specific that you've experienced with Jamie and link it to a positive quality that could help Jamie in his future in high school, college and/or career, and life)."
Words of Encouragement

"I'm calling you to share something that I've noticed a few times this week. Jamie has been texting on his phone during class time. First, I asked him if everything was OK and if there was an emergency."
Words of Accountability

"We have been discussing the difference between using their cell phones for class lessons or an emergency versus using it for personal texting, video games, listening to music, or social media. Cell phones can be a great tool for learning in class, but they can also be a huge distraction for students' learning. I'm reaching out to you to make you aware of this issue and to let you know I'm concerned it could impact Jamie's learning."
Words of Guidance

"I wanted to mention this to you and ask you to talk with Jamie about the proper use of a cell phone in our class, so we can have the best learning environment in our classroom for everyone—including Jamie."
Words of Unity

"Please let me know if you have any questions at all. My hope is for all our students to feel safe, enjoy school, learn as much as they can every day, and be ready for high school and life (use this with middle school students) or college and/or career and life (use this with high school students)."

Words of Hope

## WHAT DO GREAT TEACHERS SAY WHEN…?

**A Student is Off-task, Playing a Video Game, Watching a Video, or Watching a Movie on His Phone/Computer. (Scenario 5.2)**

### GTL Reminders to Self:

*Remember…* When students are on their phone or computer playing a video game, watching a video, or watching a movie, they seem to be in the device. The device has their undivided attention.

Words of Understanding

*Remember…* It will take time for students to make the cognitive shift away from their device and back to the lesson. They will need your patience and guidance.

Words of Grace

*Remember…* Technology has a strong magnetic pull.

Words of Guidance

*Remember…* Technology can be so entertaining for our students, and we can use video games, videos, and movies to enhance our lessons and make our lessons more engaging.

Words of Hope

*Remember…* Take every opportunity to have one-on-one conversations with all of your students. Engaging them in more face-to-face conversations, away from technology, will help them socially now and in their future.

Words of Love

*Remember…* Most middle school and high school students enjoy socializing with their peers online. Consider providing time during your class for students to socialize face-to-face with each other.

Words of Relationship

*Remember…* Encourage your students to enjoy the benefits of their devices.

Words of Encouragement

*Remember…* Encourage your students to minimize their screen time for their eye health.

Words of Encouragement

**GTL to Share with Students:**

"I know you enjoy playing video games, watching videos or movies on your phone/computer. I enjoy playing video games, watching videos, or movies on my phone/computer, too."

Words of Relationship

"But right now isn't the best time for that."

Words of Accountability

"It looks like there's something interesting on your phone/computer, but now isn't the time for looking at it. The whole class will have a break in a few minutes, and you can watch it then."

Words of Love

"Remember our class expectations about using phones/computers during class? If it's an emergency, please let me know and you can use it. If it's not an emergency, please put it away so you can get back to our lesson."
Words of Respect

(Shared with the whole class) "I understand how technology has this magnetic pull and how you can easily get distracted with playing video games and watching videos or movies on your phone/computer."
Words of Understanding

"Let's discuss the school's policy about proper cell phone and computer use in the classroom and why we have this policy." (Discuss your school's cell phone and computer use policy with the whole class.)
Words of Accountability

(Shared with the whole class) "I'm going to provide everyone some time away from our devices and our screens for our eye health. We'll take a break from our screens to socialize face-to-face with each other."
Words of Relationship

## WHAT DO GREAT TEACHERS SAY WHEN…?

**A Student is Off-task and Listening to Music on His/Her Phone (Using Ear Buds). (Scenario 5.3)**

### GTL Reminders to Self:

*Remember…* Music appeals to many of your middle school and high school students. Consider allowing your students to listen to music at the appropriate time.
Words of Relationship

*Remember…* When students are on their phone listening to their music, they are immersed in their music, and it has their undivided attention.
Words of Guidance

*Remember…* It will take time for students to make the cognitive shift and emotional shift away from their music and back to the lesson. They will need your patience and guidance.
Words of Grace

*Remember…* Music has a strong attraction to the heart and the mind.
Words of Understanding

*Remember…* Music can enhance our lessons and make our lessons more engaging.
Words of Hope

*Remember…* Take every opportunity to have one-on-one conversations with all of your students. Engage them in face-to-face conversations about their favorite music and musicians.
Words of Love

**GTL to Share with Students:**

"In our class when you are doing independent work you can listen to music as long as you stay on task and are able to complete your assignment."
Words of Accountability

"I know you enjoy listening to your music. I enjoy listening to music, too."
Words of Relationship

"But right now isn't the best time for that."
Words of Accountability

"It looks like you're listening to some music you like, but now isn't the time for listening to it. The whole class will have a break in a few minutes, and you can listen to it then."

Words of Love

"Remember our class expectations about listening to music during class? If you are doing independent work, it's OK to listen to music as long as you stay on task and are able to complete your assignment. If we're not doing independent work, please remember to put it away."

Words of Respect

(Shared with the whole class) "I understand how music has this magnetic pull and how you can easily get distracted with listening to it on your phone."

Words of Understanding

"Let's discuss the school's policy about listening to music in the classroom and why we have this policy." (With the whole class, discuss your school's policy on listening to music in the classroom.)

Words of Accountability

(Shared with the whole class) "We're going to take a break from the lesson and allow you some time on your devices to listen to music, etc."

Words of Relationship

(One-on-one conversation with student) "I noticed during break you were listening to music. What do you listen to? What do you like?"

Words of Relationship

## WHAT DO GREAT TEACHERS SAY WHEN...?

**A Student is Off-task and Searching Online for Personal Reasons. (Scenario 5.4)**

### GTL Reminders to Self:

*Remember…* Having the ability to search online for information and find it in seconds is an awesome tool for your middle school and high school students. However, this tool comes with challenges when students want to search online for personal reasons during class.

Words of Guidance

*Remember…* When students are off-task and searching online for personal reasons, they are immersed in their computer or phone, and it has their undivided attention.

Words of Guidance

*Remember…* It will take time for students to make the cognitive shift and emotional shift away from their online search for personal reasons and shift back to the lesson. They will need your patience and guidance.

Words of Grace

*Remember…* Searching and exploring new things online can feel easy, satisfying, and fun.

Words of Understanding

*Remember…* Using online resources can enhance our lessons and make our lessons more engaging.

Words of Hope

*Remember…* By proactively circulating around your classroom and paying attention to the needs of your students, you can prevent students from searching online for personal reasons.

Words of Understanding

*Remember...* Some students will choose to search online for personal reasons during class and will disengage from the lesson, and they will need to be respectfully redirected back to the lesson.

Words of Grace

### GTL to Share with Students:

"It looks like you're off-task and searching online, and now isn't the time for that."

Words of Accountability

"Remember our class expectations about searching online for personal reasons during class? If it's related to our lesson, please let me know and you can use it. If it's not related, please put it away so you can get back to our lesson."

Words of Respect

(Shared with the whole class) "I understand how technology has this magnetic pull and how you can easily get distracted with searching online."

Words of Understanding

(Shared with the whole class) "All of us are going to find ourselves getting distracted and wanting to search for something online. I want to encourage you all to focus on our lesson and put the devices away until later."

Words of High Expectations

"Let's discuss the school's policy about searching online for personal reasons in the classroom and why we have this policy." (With the whole class, discuss your school's policy on searching online for personal reasons.)

Words of Accountability

## WHAT DO GREAT TEACHERS SAY WHEN...?

**A Student is Plagiarizing Other People's Work and/Or Copying Answers from Online Sources. (Scenario 5.5)**

### GTL Reminders to Self:

*Remember...* It's going to be important for you to have a whole class conversation about why it's important for students to cite the sources they use for their academic work. First of all, citing sources gives credit to the author who wrote or created the information. Second, when we don't cite our sources properly, it miscommunicates to others we are taking the credit for what someone else has written or created. Third, it miscommunicates to the teacher what you've actually learned about the material and what you've actually written.

Words of Guidance

*Remember...* It's important to encourage middle school and high school students to show you what *they* have learned and what *they* know about the material on the assignment or on the test.

Words of Encouragement

*Remember...* Credible online information can be so helpful for middle school and high school students. Guide them in the proper use of the information to encourage the development of integrity and authentic learning.

Words of Guidance

*Remember...* Take every opportunity to have one-on-one conversations with all of your students about their work. Engaging them in face-to-face conversations will give them an opportunity to share what they have learned and know about the course material.

Words of Love

*Remember…* Online resources are plentiful and easy to access. The temptation will be out there online to find the answers and take the easy way, but our goal is to encourage students to start making these important life choices to learn it for themselves now so it will help them in the future.

Words of Understanding

*Remember…* Some middle school and high students may choose to search online for answers to questions on their class assignments, and they will need to be respectfully reminded that you want to see what *they* know about this assignment.

Words of Grace

**GTL to Share with Students:**

"As you search for information on today's assignment, let's talk about why it's important for you all to cite the sources you use for your academic work. First of all, citing sources correctly gives credit to the author who wrote or created the information. Second, when you don't cite your sources properly, it miscommunicates to others that you are taking the credit for what someone else has written or created. Third, it miscommunicates to me, your teacher what you've actually learned about the material and what you've actually written."

Words of Guidance

"I want to know what *you've* learned and what *you* know about this material."

Words of Encouragement

"The goal of this assignment and all of our assignments is for you to learn the material for yourself and then share what you have learned."

Words of High Expectations

(Privately to student to reinforce positive behavior) "I like the way you cited this author and his work in your assignment. His words support the main topic of your paper."
                                  Words of Relationship

"Holding ourselves accountable for doing the work ourselves is a great sign of integrity."
                                  Words of Accountability

"Let's discuss the school's policy about academic integrity and why we have this policy." (Discuss your school's academic integrity policy with the whole class.)
                                  Words of Accountability

(Shared with the whole class) "I understand how searching online for possible answers to the questions on this assignment is possible. The temptation might be out there online to find the answers and take the easy way, but I really want to encourage you to start making these important life choices about how you are going to learn this material to help you now and for your future. I want to encourage all of you to show me what you personally know about each question."
                                  Words of Understanding

## GTL Classroom Activities to Transform Middle School and High School Student Behavior and Your Classroom Culture

### GTL Classroom Activities for Proper Use of Technology and Devices in the Middle School and High School Classroom

We see these activities as either "in the moment" or a time to pull your students together for classroom conversations to encourage student voice and student engagement in your classroom.

We see the teacher as a facilitator and co-learner during these GTL activities and students as active participants in learning how to "see the classroom through the lens of the teacher" and how to manage their own current behavior for success and their future behavior as they get ready for high school, college and/or a career.

1. (Role-Play GTL Scenario for students who are using technology and off-task from the lesson by, for example, texting during class, watching a video during class, and listening to music during class.) Select one student to role-play a teacher and one student to role-play a student who is using technology and off-task from the lesson. Ask the role-playing student to decide which off-task technology they are going to demonstrate. Allow time for the role-playing teacher to try to address the off-task technology issue and re-engage the role-playing student in the lesson. After the first role-play, ask the off-task student who was using technology if what the role-playing teacher said was helpful. Encourage the other students in the class to help the role-playing teacher with what to say and how to respectfully respond to the off-task student using technology so they will re-engage in class. Continue the role-play activity with the other student scenarios related to off-task students using technology. Conclude each role-playing activity with a discussion of how you, as the teacher, will respectfully engage students who are using technology and off-task in your classroom.

2. (Hit the Pause Button for Discussion on Student Behavior Expectations Related to Academic Integrity and the Proper Use of Online Sources to Support Their Learning.) Share with the students that you are going to "Hit the Pause Button" on the lesson and take important time to discuss the school policies related to academic integrity and the proper use of online sources to support their learning. Explain to students the following reasons why it's important for them to cite the sources they use for their academic work: (1) citing sources correctly gives credit to the author who wrote or created the information; (2) when you don't cite your sources properly, it

miscommunicates to others that you are taking the credit for what someone else has written or created; and (3) it miscommunicates to me, your teacher, what you've actually learned about the material and what you've actually written. Ask students to share the challenges and temptations they might experience with online sources when they are completing your course assignments. Allow time for each student to share one of their challenges and/or temptations with the class. Discuss why these academic integrity policies are important and how the goal is to ensure their academic success now and for their future. Conclude the discussion by encouraging your students to reach out to you when they start to experience challenges with the course assignments, so you can support them, and they can learn the information for themselves and experience personal academic success.

3. (Getting Ready for Life Discussion about the Benefits and Challenges of Using Technology and Making Great Choices) Share with the students that you're about to have a Getting Ready for Life Discussion related to the benefits and challenges of using technology and making great choices. Explain to students how technology provides so many amazing benefits and how it is also potentially negative and harmful to us. Break the class up into small discussion groups. First, ask students to think about some of their favorite benefits of using technology and some of the potentially negative and harmful experiences they've had using technology and share them with their small group. Then ask the students to share their success stories—what they've done in the past to make great choices to prevent the potentially negative or harmful use of technology. Circulate around the classroom to listen in on the small group discussions. Allow time for students to share these success stories for making great choices in their small group. Bring the whole class back together and ask if any group wants to share with the whole class. Remind students how their personal success stories might help and encourage other students to

overcome the same or similar challenges with technology. Conclude the discussion by sharing how making great choices and using technology for its benefits and preventing the potentially negative or harmful technology use will set them up for success in high school, college and/or career, and life.

# 6

# What Do Great Teachers Say When a Student is an Attention Seeker?

What do you say when a student is disrupting class and is constantly wanting to be seen and/or heard (e.g., Class Entertainer, Social Butterfly, Social Influencer, and Excessive Talker). This chapter provides teacher-friendly charts with Great Teacher Language (GTL) Reminders to Self, GTL to Share with Students, GTL to Use When Talking and Communicating with Parents, and GTL Classroom Activities specifically related to the following:

- **Scenario 6.1**: A Student is Intentionally Asking Questions to Distract the Teacher Away From the Lesson.
- **Scenario 6.2**: A Student Is Up Out of His/Her Seat, Looking at Another Student's Phone, Laughing, and Socializing with Other Students.
- **Scenario 6.3**: A Student is Annoying Another Student and Wanting Their Attention Either Verbally, in Writing, Or by Texting.
- **Scenario 6.4**: A Student is Being the Class Entertainer and/or Social Influencer.
- **Scenario 6.5**: A Student is Verbally Monopolizing the Lesson by Answering Every Question or Constantly Asking Questions.
- **Scenario 6.6**: A Student is Constantly Talking with Other Students During the Lesson.

> We know these are not the only attention-seeking behaviors that happen in your classroom. These specific scenarios are a starting point for you to develop your GTL for your classroom. For some of our student behavior scenarios, we have included GTL examples for you to use when talking with parents. These GTL examples are templates for phone conversations, emails, or other types of messages to develop strong communication between teachers and parents and to promote understanding, relationships, trust, and collaboration.

Every middle school and high school student in your classroom needs attention. Some of them need assistance with academic challenges; others need help with social challenges. The greatest attention seekers in your classroom are relentless in their pursuit. They seem to want attention from everyone, all the time. Many of these students find great pleasure in socializing at school. They talk excessively and try to entertain or influence other students throughout the day. Others try to gain attention by policing the class and telling the teacher everything that's done wrong. Their behaviors are not usually malicious; however, they are not learning, they often annoy other students, and they disrupt class and impede learning. Your Language of Practice (LoP) in the form of GTL can offer these attention-seeking middle school and high school students the accountability, encouragement, grace, guidance, high expectations, hope, love, relationships, respect, understanding, and unity they need and provide redirection for their actions in school and for their future. Your words and actions will show the other students how to relate and respond to these attention seekers.

Let's face it. Sometimes middle school and high school students who need extra attention can be challenging. Why do some students need more attention than others? Giving appropriate attention to any student in your classroom starts with separating the student from their behavior. With attention seekers, it's important to look beyond the aggravation and share an attitude of grace, love, understanding, and accountability which conveys "You are worth my time and undivided attention, I want to understand what you need, but right now is not the time for us to talk." These students need accountability for their behavior, and they also need your individual attention and some quality time. They need to know you care. They need your eye contact and your respectful attention, and they need to know you are listening to them. Your actions and words demonstrate to them you are interested in who they are, what they are doing, and what they need.

Many of the discipline issues in the middle school and high school classroom can be addressed with quality time. Yet we often feel like there aren't enough hours in the day to pay attention to each student individually. However, when we spend just a few minutes of quality time listening attentively to a student, it can fill their need for attention and give us insight into how we can redirect their misbehavior or meet their individual need.

Sometimes an insatiable appetite for attention prevents attention seekers from seeing the detrimental effects of their behavior. Class entertainers display silly and immature behaviors. Social butterflies and social influencers often distract and annoy other students. Without the proper guidance and accountability, these misbehaviors can have negative long-term consequences. Our job is to help middle school and high school attention seekers minimize their extreme need for attention and replace it with an increased self-awareness and personal accountability that positively impacts their learning and success in school and in their future.

Attention seekers are seeking affirmation from others. Class entertainers want laughs, while social butterflies and social influencers want to "know and be known." To satisfy their appetite for attention, teachers can help these students channel their energies into more productive efforts. For example, class entertainers can get laughs and applause performing in the school play. Social butterflies and social influencers can network in school clubs and other extracurricular activities. Our language can provide the guidance and direction that these students need to encourage and ensure their success in school and in their future.

We can promote unity and teamwork in our classroom by modeling to all middle school and high school students that everyone deserves our respect. If teachers are not careful, our words and actions can demonstrate to students that we don't like the attention seekers. Our goal is for students to learn, and attention seekers can often deter learning. The way we talk *about* attention seekers and the way we talk *to* them show how we feel about them. Students can misinterpret our words and actions. If students think our words and actions indicate a certain dislike for a student, the other students may feel they have the right to feel and act the same way. It is so important to carefully deal with attention seekers while maintaining the unity within our classroom.

What do you say to help guide attention seekers from socially unacceptable behaviors to socially acceptable behaviors in the classroom? When we hold middle school and high school students accountable for inappropriate behavior while maintaining their dignity, students observe grace and poise in action and learn a valuable life lesson about how to treat others. It helps them understand that inappropriate behavior does not dictate whether or not we show someone respect.

---

### WHAT DO GREAT TEACHERS SAY WHEN...?

**A Student is Intentionally Asking Questions to Distract the Teacher Away From the Lesson. (Scenario 6.1)**

#### GTL Reminders to Self:

*Remember…* It might seem easier in the short term to give in to middle school and high school students and let them have their way—but they need structured accountability and someone to hold them accountable for their words and actions.

Words of Accountability

*Remember…* When you harbor feelings of resentment and frustration, it can impact your ability to see the students' real needs.

Words of Grace

*Remember…* Classroom experiences can be some of the most influential experiences of a student's life—make sure those experiences are positive and uplifting for all students!

Words of Hope

*Remember…* Some students are clever and are performing for other students and want to distract you from delivering the lesson content and assignments.

Words of Guidance

*Remember…* Consider reminding students to stay focused on the lesson and to make sure the questions they ask are related to the content being taught.

Words of High Expectations

*Remember…* When a student asks a question that distracts you from the lesson, respectfully ask the student to jot the question down for a discussion with you later after class.

Words of Respect

**GTL to Share with Students:**

"This just isn't the time for those questions right now, but I am really interested in the questions you just asked. As soon as we're finished with this activity, we will talk about them."

Words of Relationship

"I am sorry—I didn't realize you had a problem. Sometimes it may take me a while to understand what you are wanting to say or what you need."

Words of Understanding

"Those are great questions, but let's park those for right now and stay focused on the lesson. We'll circle back to those questions after the lesson."

*Words of Love*

(Shared with the whole class to reinforce positive behavior) "Those are great questions—they are relevant and related to what we're discussing. Thank you."

*Words of Encouragement*

(Shared with the whole class to encourage relevant questions) "Now that we've gone through the lesson, does anyone have any questions related to the material we've discussed today?"

*Words of Unity*

(One-on-one conversation with student to reinforce positive behavior) "I noticed you were focused on our lesson today. Do you have any questions you want to ask me about today's lesson?"

*Words of Relationship*

## WHAT DO GREAT TEACHERS SAY WHEN…?

**A Student Is Up Out of His/Her Seat, Looking at Another Student's Phone, Laughing, and Socializing with Other Students. (Scenario 6.2)**

### GTL Reminders to Self:

*Remember…* Don't forget to call parents when things are going well. Yes, parents of middle school and high school students would love to get a positive phone call concerning their child!

*Words of Encouragement*

*Remember…* When we allow the same misbehavior to go on and on without accountability, we send the unintentional message that we do not expect the students to meet the guidelines and high expectations for our classroom.
Words of Accountability

*Remember…* Rather than harboring ill feelings for misbehaving students like the social butterfly and social influencer, demonstrate grace to them and dig deep to get at the root of the problem to better understand their behaviors.
Words of Grace

*Remember…* There might be times when your middle school and high school students are off-task and distracting others from learning. This behavior may be a signal that they need extra attention for instructional or emotional reasons. When you give them extra attention, you are showing them they are important to you.
Words of Love

*Remember…* Students need to have an outlet, so consider allowing them opportunities to talk and socialize in your class.
Words of Understanding

**GTL to Share with Students:**

(Sharing with the whole class) "If you are out of your seat and distracting other students, I promise I won't single you out or raise my voice. I will quietly and respectfully make eye contact with you, tap you on the shoulder, and remind you to go to your seat."
Words of Respect

"If you have something you would like to share with someone else, please wait until we finish the lesson

and then you will have the opportunity to discuss what you have to say."
Words of Guidance

"When you're out of your seat, it disrupts the lesson. You're not learning, and it keeps the other students from learning, too."
Words of Accountability

(Talking to student alone) "I'm concerned about what you have been doing in your other classes. I hear you are up out of your seat, talking all the time, disrupting class. You can do better than that—I know you can. We've all seen the amazing changes you've made in our class!"
Words of High Expectations

(Privately to the student) "I noticed you came into class and got to work right away. Great job!"
Words of Encouragement

### GTL to Use When Talking and Communicating with Parents:

**Positive and proactive phone call to encourage parents and celebrate student behavior.**

(A middle school or high school student is learning how to come into class and get to work quietly and quickly. This improved behavior is paying off with improved grades, and you want to share a positive update with his parents.)

(Note: This GTL phone conversation provides a template you can modify and send to parents as a letter, email, text message, etc.).

"Hello! My name is…. I'm Jamie's teacher. He's not in trouble. Is now a good time for us to talk?"
Words of Respect

"I enjoy having Jamie in my class. He is… (share something personal, positive, and specific that you've experienced with Jamie and link it to a positive quality that could help Jamie in his future in high school, college and/or career, and life)."

Words of Encouragement

"I'm calling you to share some great news about Jamie and how he's been doing in class. He's been coming into class and getting right to work quietly and quickly. His improved behavior is also paying off with improved grades, and I was excited to share it with you!"

Words of Hope

"We've been talking in class about the importance of learning life skills for success now and in their future. So I've been telling students about the importance of coming into class—just like they might go into a job one day—and get right to work, and Jamie has been doing that."

Words of Guidance

"I'm really proud of Jamie and wanted to share it with you."

Words of Encouragement

"Please let me know if you have any questions at all. My hope is for all our students to feel safe, enjoy school, learn as much as they can every day, and be ready for high school and life (use this with middle school students) or college and/or career and life (use this with high school students)."

Words of Hope

## WHAT DO GREAT TEACHERS SAY WHEN…?

**A Student is Annoying Another Student and Wanting Their Attention Either Verbally, in Writing, Or by Texting. (Scenario 6.3)**

### GTL Reminders to Self:

*Remember…* Teach your students the difference between the right kind of reporting and the wrong kind of reporting. The wrong kind of reporting is saying something to the teacher to gain attention or just to get someone else in trouble. The right kind of reporting is sharing information with the teacher that helps the student, keeps trouble from happening, or helps someone else. The goal of the right kind of reporting is to maintain a safe classroom environment for all students.

Words of Guidance

*Remember…* Circulate and pay attention to students who are annoying other students verbally, in writing, or with texting and be ready to address the situation.

Words of Accountability

*Remember…* Try to get to know every one of your middle school and high school students and why they act the way they do.

Words of Relationship

*Remember…* Some students need to be taught how to interact with others. We can rehearse, role-play, and model good behavior and discuss the issue together.

Words of Guidance

*Remember…* Sometimes students are wanting to get the attention of another student because they might like them and want to get to know them better, but these students need to respect the other student's boundaries.

Words of Respect

*Remember…* Take every opportunity to have one-on-one conversations with all of your students. Engage them in face-to-face conversations to get to know them better and offer them your individual attention.

Words of Love

**GTL to Share with Students:**

(Shared with the whole class) "There's a difference between the right kind of reporting and the wrong kind of reporting. The wrong kind of reporting is saying something to the teacher to gain attention or just to get someone else in trouble. The right kind of reporting is sharing information with the teacher that helps the student, keeps trouble from happening, or helps someone else. The goal of the right kind of reporting is to maintain a safe classroom environment for everyone."

Words of Guidance

"Let me stop what I'm doing because I want to listen to you and find out what's really happening with you and the other student."

Words of Understanding

"If you are just trying to get someone in trouble, you need to rethink what you want to tell me."

Words of Guidance

"When someone is annoying you, you should confidently and politely ask that person to stop. If he doesn't stop, let me know."

Words of Guidance

(Talking privately to both students) "Jamie, I appreciate your respectfully sharing your frustrations with me. Let's talk about how each of you sees this situation. I want to hear from both of you about what's going on."

Words of Understanding

"If another student continues to annoy you, please let me know as soon as possible. Let's address your concerns openly, honestly, respectfully, and as quickly as possible."

Words of Grace

"Remember, before you choose to annoy someone, ask yourself, 'How would I feel if someone were treating me like that?'"

Words of Guidance

## WHAT DO GREAT TEACHERS SAY WHEN…?

**A Student is Being the Class Entertainer and/or Social Influencer. (Scenario 6.4)**

### GTL Reminders to Self:

*Remember…* There is a reason why middle school and high school students act the way they do, so find out what's going on and what is driving those behaviors.

Words of Understanding

*Remember…* All students are so different and so interesting in their own way. Some of them are outgoing and some of them are quiet. Find ways to get to know each student better. You can learn a lot from their differences.

Words of Understanding

*Remember…* Rather than harboring ill feelings for misbehaving students like the class entertainer and/or social influencer, demonstrate grace to them and dig deep to get at the root of the problem to better understand their behaviors.

Words of Grace

*Remember…* Be aware of the social influencers in your class. These students can often influence other students to make either positive or negative choices.
Words of Guidance

*Remember…* Class entertainers and social influencers can have strong personalities that can lead to positive school experiences or negative school experiences, and they need proper accountability, guidance, and respect.
Words of Understanding

*Remember…* To satisfy their appetite for attention, you can help class entertainers and social influencers to channel their energies into more productive efforts. For example, class entertainers can get laughs and applause performing in the school play. Social influencers can network in school clubs and other extracurricular activities.
Words of High Expectations

### GTL to Share with Students:

"You are not in trouble, but we need to have a heart-to-heart conversation about your behavior."
Words of Accountability

"There's a time for work and a time for play."
Words of Guidance

"You really need to try out for the school play—you would be great!"
Words of Encouragement

"Have you ever thought about serving as an officer in a school club? You certainly have the leadership skills to do it!"
Words of Encouragement

(Privately with student) "When you're trying to entertain the class, that makes it hard for students to stay focused on the lesson. You're not learning, and it keeps the other students from learning, too."
Words of Accountability

(Privately with student) "We have a new student in class. Could you help them find their way around school and introduce them to some students?"
Words of Relationship

(Privately to the student) "I saw you in the school play last night, and you were amazing! I can see you being an actress one day."
Words of Encouragement

(Privately to the student) "I heard you were elected as an officer for your club! Congratulations! You have the skills to be a great leader, and I'm excited to see your leadership in our school and where your leadership skills will take you in your future."
Words of Encouragement

**GTL to Use When Talking and Communicating With Parents:**

**Phone call to build trust with the parent and inform them of their student's behavior in class: The student is distracting the class by trying to entertain others and make people laugh, which warrants a call to their parent.**

(Note: This GTL phone conversation provides a template you can modify and send to parents as a letter, email, text message, etc.).

"Hello! My name is…. I'm Jamie's teacher. He's not in trouble. Is now a good time for us to talk?"
Words of Respect

"I enjoy having Jamie in my class. He is… (share something personal, positive, and specific that you've

experienced with Jamie and link it to a positive quality that could help Jamie in his future in high school, college and/or career, and life)."
Words of Encouragement

"I'm calling you to share something that's been happening at school. Jamie has a terrific personality and is liked by other students in our class. He has been trying to make students laugh in class, and it disrupts class and gets us off-track from the lesson, and the students can't focus, and it's starting to negatively impact Jamie's own learning and his grades in this class."
Words of Accountability

"I wanted to mention this to you and work with you on a plan for addressing this issue, so we can have the best learning environment in the classroom for everyone—including Jamie."
Words of Unity

"As I mentioned to you earlier, Jamie has a lot of potential, and I can imagine him using his personality and strengths to be whatever he wants to be in his future. I really want to make sure we're doing everything we—you, Jamie, and I—can to address these class disruptions so he can experience success now and in his future."
Words of Hope

"Do you have any questions or thoughts about it right now?
Words of Understanding

"Please let me know if you have any questions at all. My hope is for all our students to feel safe, enjoy school, learn as much as they can every day, and be ready for high school and life (use this with middle school students) or college and/or career and life (use this with high school students)."
Words of Hope

## WHAT DO GREAT TEACHERS SAY WHEN…?

**A Student is Verbally Monopolizing the Lesson by Answering Every Question or Constantly Asking Questions. (Scenario 6.5)**

### GTL Reminders to Self:

*Remember…* The questions that students ask can provide tremendous insight into how much they trust you—and how safe they feel in your classroom.
Words of Relationship

*Remember…* Sometimes using "you" messages can place blame, whereas using "I" messages can be a more respectful way of expressing your emotions without blame while holding the student accountable.
Words of Accountability

*Remember…* One way that some middle school and high school students learn is by asking questions and verbally processing information. Their questions can help them and the other students understand the lesson better. However, sometimes students' questions are irrelevant, unnecessary, not on topic, or for attention. These students need guidance in how to ask acceptable questions.
Words of Understanding

*Remember…* When students feel free to ask questions, it provides a classroom environment that fosters creativity and learning.
Words of Guidance

*Remember…* Some of your students monopolize the lesson by asking questions because they are feeling pressure and need your affirmation as they strive to make higher grades for their future college plans.
Words of Understanding

*Remember...* When these students try to monopolize the lesson, there are some passively disengaged students who need your encouragement to engage in the lesson.

Words of Encouragement

### GTL to Share with Students:

(Shared with the whole class) "I want everyone to feel free to ask questions in our class to encourage creativity and learning."

Words of Guidance

(Shared with the whole class) "Let's talk about our different learning styles. We all learn in different ways. Some of us learn better by talking and asking questions. Some of us learn better by listening and thinking quietly. Some of us learn better by being physically active, moving around, and participating in activities. Some of us learn better by reading and writing quietly. We're all different and we'll be seeing these different learning styles in each other."

Words of Relationship

(Talking privately with the student) "You're not in trouble, but we need to have a heart-to-heart conversation about how important it is to let other students have an opportunity to answer questions and feel successful."

Words of Accountability

(Privately with the student) "I want to hear what you have to ask, and I am interested in your questions, so jot those questions down on a Post-it note and put them on our Parking Lot board for later."

Words of Guidance

"Those questions, right now, are not about our lesson. I'm glad you're interested in asking questions, and we can talk about them after class. Right now, it would be more helpful to focus your questions on our class work."

Words of Accountability

(Privately to student to reinforce positive behavior) "I noticed you let other students answer questions today. What a great example for other students to follow."

Words of Encouragement

(Whispering to student) "I appreciate how you waited to raise your hand and gave the other students your attention while they were speaking. Great job of showing respect."

Words of Respect

## WHAT DO GREAT TEACHERS SAY WHEN…?

**A Student is Constantly Talking with Other Students During the Lesson. (Scenario 6.6)**

### GTL Reminders to Self:

*Remember…* There are going to be days that you don't like what your middle school or high school students do, like constant talking, but they still need you to care about them and hold them accountable for those actions.

Words of Love

*Remember…* Rather than harboring ill feelings for misbehaving students like the constant talker, grant them grace and dig deep to get at the root of the problem to better understand their behaviors.

Words of Grace

*Remember…* There might be times when your students are talking and distracting others from learning. This behavior may be a signal that they need extra attention for instructional or emotional reasons. When you give them extra attention, you are showing them they are important to you.

Words of Understanding

*Remember…* Students need to have an outlet, so allow them opportunities to talk and socialize during your class.

Words of Understanding

*Remember…* Some students get energy by talking with other students, so try to incorporate group work to give them time to talk to others about the lesson.

Words of Relationship

*Remember…* Group work is important for middle school and high school students. It allows them to practice teamwork and collaboration and prepare for work teams later in life.

Words of Relationship

*Remember…* Some students might be verbal processors and feel the need to talk to others about what they are learning.

Words of Guidance

### GTL to Share with Students:

(Talking privately with the student) "You're not in trouble, but we need to have a heart-to-heart conversation about how important it is to listen as we learn together in class."

Words of Accountability

(Whispering to a student) "I've noticed you were talking to another student while I was teaching. Is everything OK?"
Words of Love

(Shared with the whole class) "I want everyone to feel free to talk and share in our class to encourage participation in the lesson so we can learn from each other."
Words of Unity

"I know you enjoy talking with your friends. I enjoy talking with my friends, too."
Words of Relationship

"But this isn't the right time for that."
Words of Accountability

"I'm going to give you a minute to make the mental shift back to what we're doing."
Words of Guidance

(Privately to student to reinforce positive behavior) "I appreciate how you listened during our class today. Great job of showing respect."
Words of Respect

**GTL to Use When Talking and Communicating With Parents:**

**Phone call to build trust with the parent and inform them of their student's behavior in class: The student is distracting the class by constantly talking with other students, which warrants a call to their parent.**

(Note: This GTL phone conversation provides a template you can modify and send to parents as a letter, email, text message, etc.).

"Hello! My name is…. I'm Jamie's teacher. He's not in trouble. Is now a good time for us to talk?"
Words of Respect

"I enjoy having Jamie in my class. He is… (share something personal, positive, and specific that you've experienced with Jamie and link it to a positive quality that could help Jamie in his future in high school, college and/or career, and life)."

                                  Words of Encouragement

"I'm calling you to share something that's been happening at school. Jamie has a terrific personality and is liked by other students in our class. He has been constantly talking with other students, and it disrupts class and gets us off-track from the lesson, and the students can't focus, and it's starting to negatively impact Jamie's own learning and his grades in this class."

                                  Words of Accountability

"I wanted to mention this to you and work with you on a plan for addressing this issue, so we can have the best learning environment in the classroom for everyone—including Jamie."

                                            Words of Unity

"As I mentioned to you earlier, Jamie has a lot of potential, and I can imagine him using his personality and strengths to be whatever he wants to be in his future. I really want to make sure we're doing everything we—you, Jamie, and I—can to address these class disruptions so he can experience success now and in his future."

                                          Words of Hope

"Do you have any questions or thoughts about it right now?"

                                  Words of Understanding

"Please let me know if you have any questions at all. My hope is for all our students to feel safe, enjoy school, learn as much as they can every day, and be

> ready for high school and life (use this with middle school students) or college and/or career and life (use this with high school students)."
>
> Words of Hope

## GTL Classroom Activities to Transform Middle School and High School Student Behavior and Your Classroom Culture

### GTL Classroom Activities for Attention Seekers in Middle School and High School

We see these activities as either "in the moment" or a time to pull your students together for classroom conversations to encourage student voice and student engagement in your classroom.

We see the teacher as a facilitator and co-learner during these GTL activities and students as active participants in learning how to "see the classroom through the lens of the teacher" and how to manage their own current behavior for success and their future behavior as they get ready for high school, college and/or a career.

1. (Role-Play GTL Scenario for students to help them practice how to respectfully respond to another student who is distracting them in class by, for example, trying to make them laugh, talking to them constantly, and asking them questions). Select one student to role-play a student and another student to role-play a student who is distracting the other student from the lesson. Ask the role-playing student who is distracting the other student to decide which distracting behavior they are going to demonstrate. Allow time for the role-playing student to try to respectfully respond to the distracting student. After the first role-play, ask the role-playing student who was distracting other students if what the role-playing student said was helpful and respectful. Encourage the other students in the class to help the role-playing student with what to say and how to respectfully respond

to the role-playing student who is distracting. Continue the role-play activity with new role-players and use the other student-distracting scenarios. Conclude each role-playing activity with a discussion of how you, as the teacher, will respectfully engage students who are distracting other students in your classroom.

2. (Hit the Pause Button for Discussion on Student Behavior Expectations and Communicating with Parents to Build Trust and Support Student Learning) Share with the students that you are going to "Hit the Pause Button" on the lesson and take important time to discuss the school policies related to communicating with parents and your plan for communicating with their parents to build trust and support student learning. Share with students the importance of maintaining communication with their parents even as they are becoming more independent as middle school and high school students. Explain to students why you will reach out to parents (1) to share positive updates, (2) to build trust and a positive relationship, (3) to get their help and support from time to time, (4) to keep them informed of your progress, (5) to invite them to school activities, and (6) to get their insight into how to support your learning better. Ask the students if they have any questions about these reasons for communicating with their parents. Allow time for students to discuss their questions and concerns about communicating with their parents. Conclude the discussion by encouraging your students and sharing with them how excited you are to get to know their parents and build a positive relationship with them. Explain how these positive relationships will promote unity and their success in middle school and high school.

3. (Getting Ready for Life Discussion about Linking Their Interests and Strengths to Middle School and High School Extra-Curricular and Co-Curricular Activities and Making Great Choices) Share with the students that you're about to have a Getting Ready for Life discussion related to linking their individual interests and strengths

to extra-curricular and co-curricular activities at your school and making great choices. Explain to students how your school offers many extra-curricular and co-curricular activities to help them grow in their strengths and pursue their personal interests. Share a list of your school's extracurricular and co-curricular activities with your students. Then, break the class into small discussion groups. First, ask students to share their personal strengths and interests with their small group. Then, ask the students to consider the list of extra-curricular and co-curricular activities and share possible school activities they could be a part of that are linked to their personal strengths and interests. Circulate around the classroom to listen in on the small group discussions. Allow time for students to share their personal success stories for making great choices and their positive experiences about being in an extra-curricular or co-curricular group. Bring the whole class back together and ask if any group wants to share with the whole class. Remind students how their personal success stories might help and encourage another student to pursue their interests and participate in extra-curricular and/or co-curricular activity. Conclude the discussion by sharing how making great choices and participating in extra-curricular and/or co-curricular activities will set them up for success for high school, college and/or career, and life.

# 7

# What Do Great Teachers Say When a Student Outburst Happens?

What do you say when you want to appropriately and respectfully address an inappropriate middle school or high school student outburst in your classroom? This chapter provides teacher-friendly charts with Great Teacher Language (GTL) Reminders to Self, GTL to Share with Students, GTL to Use When Talking and Communicating with Parents, and GTL Classroom Activities specifically related to:

**Scenario 7.1**: A Student Yells Out, "This Is So Boring!"
**Scenario 7.2**: A Student Yells Out, "I'm Lost! I don't Understand!"
**Scenario 7.3**: A Student Yells Out, "Why Do We Have to Do This…? When Are We Ever Going to Need This or Use This?"
**Scenario 7.4**: A Student Yells Out Profanity, "@#$%!"
**Scenario 7.5**: A Student Yells Out a Verbally Aggressive Outburst and/or Acts Out a Physically Aggressive Outburst.

> We know these are not the only outbursts that happen in your classroom. These specific scenarios are a starting point for you to develop your GTL for your classroom. For some

of our student behavior scenarios, we have included GTL examples for you to use when talking with parents. These GTL examples are templates for phone conversations, emails, or other types of messages to develop strong communication between teachers and parents and to promote understanding, relationships, trust, and collaboration.

Wanted: Uninterrupted quality time for teaching and learning. No intercom, no knocks on the door, and no student outbursts. Instructional time without distractions is a teacher's dream. It is easy to become frustrated when distractions occur. However, we need to be careful in how we deal with distractions, especially inappropriate middle school and high school student outbursts, because they affect everyone and can lead to larger problems. It's important to model appropriate responses to outbursts that respect the student, quietly redirect the student, diffuse the situation, and minimize the loss of instructional time. Your Language of Practice (LoP) in the form of GTL can offer these students the accountability, encouragement, grace, guidance, high expectations, hope, love, relationships, respect, understanding, and unity they need in the moment and beyond.

An inappropriate outburst from a middle school and high school student is like a flashing light that says, "I need your help." Such behavior is a loud and clear indication that the student is feeling upset by something and might indicate a deeper emotional issue they are experiencing. The sooner we can get to the bottom of what is troubling the student, the sooner the student can re-engage with learning. Student outbursts in the classroom can range from shouting out answers to loud disrespectful profanity or verbally aggressive and/or physically aggressive outbursts. Whatever the case, it's important to try to uncover the reason for these behaviors and address them with accountability and care. Some inappropriate outbursts can be addressed in the classroom, while other outburst behaviors may require more support from the teacher, guidance counselors, or parents for a long-term solution.

When middle school and high school student outbursts occur in the classroom, there is a tendency for us to give back to students what they give us. If they get loud, we get loud. If they get loud *and* angry, then we get loud *and* angry. It is difficult not to react with a loud voice when students are loud and even more difficult not to show anger when students are angry. An inappropriate student outburst affects everyone, and your response to it will also affect everyone. Every student in the classroom anxiously waits to see how you are going to handle the situation. They all need to see and hear us maintain the dignity of the student while we hold them accountable for their actions.

Inappropriate student outbursts demonstrate a lack of self-management. Students need us to model grace, self-management, and self-respect with our words and actions. They need to see us respond to inappropriate outbursts and stressful situations with poise and understanding. Our goal is for students to learn from our example and start demonstrating self-management behaviors that positively impact their learning and success in school and in their future.

---

### WHAT DO GREAT TEACHERS SAY WHEN...?

**A Student Yells Out, "This Is So Boring!" (Scenario 7.1)**

#### GTL Reminders to Self:

*Remember...* If middle school and high school students disrupt class, respectfully remind them the primary focus is on the learning that day.
Words of Accountability

*Remember...* It's important to keep the focus on learning and not to personalize every disruption. Let the students know how important it is for us to complete the planned lesson, activities, and group work to maximize learning.
Words of High Expectations

*Remember...* If a student is disrupting class, try to continue your teaching. Maintain the dignity of the student and hold him/her accountable by walking over and whispering to the student that you will discuss his/her behavior after class.

Words of Respect

*Remember...* No student is perfect. All of them make mistakes. Outbursts can indicate a deeper issue. Be sure to give middle school and high school students a second chance whenever possible while letting them know their behavior was not acceptable.

Words of Grace

*Remember...* Eliminating boredom in the classroom is the responsibility of both the student and the teacher.

Words of Accountability

*Remember...* Boredom is sometimes accompanied with a lack of interest in the content area you're teaching.

Words of Understanding

*Remember...* Consider having one-on-one conversations with your middle school and high school students to discover their interests and their passions.

Words of Relationship

**GTL to Share with Students:**

(Talking to the whole class) "My goal is to make what we are learning each day as interesting and relevant as possible."

Words of Encouragement

(Talking to the whole class) "If you're starting to feel bored with the lesson or have questions about it, please respectfully let me know how you're feeling about the lesson."

Words of Guidance

(Whispering to student) "Shouting during class is not a respectful way to communicate that you're bored.

I want to better understand why you're feeling bored. Let's talk about it after class."
Words of Accountability

(Talking individually to the student) "Talk to me about why you think this is so boring. I really want to know what you are thinking and how I can make it more interesting."
Words of Understanding

"I'm going to give you a minute to make the mental shift back to what we're doing."
Words of Guidance

(Whispering to student) "I don't want to single you out in front of everybody, but we need to talk after class about your behavior just now."
Words of Respect

"Help me understand why you said that?"
Words of Understanding

"I plan to have one-on-one conversations with each of you this year. I want to get to know your personal interests and your talents."
Words of Relationship

## WHAT DO GREAT TEACHERS SAY WHEN…?

**A Student Yells Out, "I'm Lost! I Don't Understand!" (Scenario 7.2)**

### GTL Reminders to Self:

*Remember…* Sometimes middle school and high school students act out because they don't understand the assignment.
Words of Understanding

*Remember…* When you start to feel frustrated, slow down, breathe, and take a few minutes to calm down. You don't want to say or do something to harm your relationship with your students.

        Words of Relationship

*Remember…* Encourage all your students to quietly and quickly let you know when they don't understand the content you're teaching.

        Words of Encouragement

*Remember…* When dealing with any discipline problem, it is essential to get to the root of the problem to better understand middle school and high school students' behaviors.

        Words of Respect

*Remember…* When students feel lost during a lesson, they can become frustrated, act out, shut down, or quit trying to understand.

        Words of Understanding

*Remember…* Every content area has a language of its own. Sometimes the language of the content area you teach resembles a foreign language to some students and they respond by shouting out about their inability to understand.

        Words of Guidance

### GTL to Share with Students:

(Shared to the whole class) "When I feel lost or confused trying to learn something new, it helps to talk to someone about it. Please let me know during or after class if you need my help, and we can talk together to help you understand."

        Words of Relationship

"Yesterday you seemed to understand this concept, but today you seem frustrated about it. How can I help you?"
Words of Understanding

"When you are confused and don't understand something in class, please remember to quietly and quickly let me know you don't understand."
Words of Guidance

"When you find yourself having a hard time with the lesson or assignments, let me know and we can talk together about it."
Words of Love

"I know these concepts are challenging—but you've almost got it—you're almost there—just hang in there for a little while longer. Let me help you with this."
Words of Hope

(Talking privately with the student) "You're not in trouble, but we need to have a heart-to-heart conversation about how to respond when you don't understand what we are doing in class. I want to help you understand."
Words of Accountability

## WHAT DO GREAT TEACHERS SAY WHEN...?

**A Student Yells Out, "Why Do We Have to Do This...? When Are We Ever Going to Need This or Use This?" (Scenario 7.3)**

### GTL Reminders to Self:

*Remember...* There are going to be days when you don't like what your middle school or high school students say, but they still need you to care for them while holding them accountable for those inappropriate outbursts.
Words of Love

*Remember…* Some middle school and high school students may not naturally understand the relevance or importance of what they are learning or how it will impact them now and in their future.

Words of Guidance

*Remember…* Encourage all your students to quietly and quickly let you know when they don't understand the purpose or relevance of the content you're teaching.

Words of Encouragement

*Remember…* Many inappropriate outbursts can be prevented by proactively surveying the classroom landscape for the needs of your students and attending to them when they need it the most.

Words of Grace

*Remember…* Helping students learn how to ask questions respectfully can promote trust, foster relationships, and optimize learning.

Words of Relationship

*Remember…* Helping students understand "The Why" of what they are learning is essential.

Words of Understanding

*Remember…* When students don't understand why they need to learn the information or how they might use it in their future, they may become frustrated, act out, shut down, or quit trying to learn.

Words of Understanding

**GTL to Share with Students:**

"It seems like you might be frustrated about today's work—let me explain why this assignment is important and how you can use it in your life."

Words of Guidance

(Whispering to student) "In the future, it would be better for you to share your frustrations with me privately and respectfully—like I'm doing right now. You can always share your frustrations about our classwork with me."

Words of Respect

(Sharing with the whole class) "Outbursts are not OK, and they disrupt class. However, I appreciate how someone asked, 'Why is this work important?' Next time, please ask me that question in private."

Words of Accountability

(Whispering to student) "Help me understand why you asked 'Why do we have to do this'? Tell me more… Is it too hard? Is it boring? I want to understand."

Words of Understanding

(Shared with the whole class) "Let's look at the effect this issue could have on you… your family… our community… etc."

Words of Relationship

(Shared with the whole class) "Let's talk about how this idea is impacting our world today."

Words of Unity

(Shared with the whole class) "This information (share something content-specific) is going to help you as you (share something specific about the link to their future in high school, college and/or career, or their future)."

Words of Hope

## WHAT DO GREAT TEACHERS SAY WHEN…?

**A Student Yells Out Profanity, "@#$%!" (Scenario 7.4)**

### GTL Reminders to Self:

*Remember…* There might be days when your middle school or high school students yell out profanity in your class. They still need you to care them while holding them accountable for those inappropriate outbursts.

Words of Accountability

*Remember…* Singling middle school or high school students out when they've demonstrated disrespect (e.g., yelling out profanity) can cause additional shame and can escalate the problem. To de-escalate the situation, respectfully ask the student to step outside in the hall to privately discuss the issue.

Words of Respect

*Remember…* When you separate the student from his/her behavior, it allows you to "take a step back" and let the student know that "I still care for you—but I don't like your behavior."

Words of Grace

*Remember…* Don't allow disrespectful student behavior to become a personal conflict—you vs. student. Keep the focus on helping the student and not on defending yourself, maintaining your power, saving face, and so on.

Words of Unity

*Remember…* When students yell out profanity, it can shock you and the other students. Your students are watching how you will react and handle the situation.

Words of Guidance

*Remember…* When you're setting up your classroom rules and behavior expectations, it's important for you to make all students aware of the school policies and consequences for the use of profanity in your classroom before it happens.

Words of Guidance

*Remember…* Share with your students and spend time discussing why profanity is not allowed at school and why choosing profanity can negatively impact their relationships, life, and future.

Words of Guidance

### GTL to Share with Students:

(Shared privately with student) "Your yelling out in class really took me by surprise—what's going on?"

Words of Understanding

(Shared privately with student) "You know, we just don't talk that way in this class. I know that something may have caused you to act that way, but we can't use that language."

Words of Accountability

(Speaking privately with student) "Your language right now was not respectful. Let's step outside in the hall to discuss the issue."

Words of Respect

(Speaking privately with student) "Help me understand why you used profanity—what happened?"

Words of Understanding

"If you find yourself having a moment when you really want to say something that you shouldn't—Stop—Think of all of the other possibilities—And choose your words carefully."

Words of Guidance

"Using profanity in our classroom is not appropriate language. Let's discuss the school policy about using profanity in our school."
Words of Guidance

(Shared with the whole class) "Here are four reasons why using profanity might negatively impact your relationships and your future: (1) it is rude, obscene, and disrespectful, and others are offended and feel disrespected hearing it; (2) it is often spoken with anger, aggression, and disrespect, so others are uncomfortable and feel unsafe hearing it; (3) it demonstrates a lack of self-control and self-management, so others are not quick to trust someone using profanity; and (4) it sometimes communicates a lack of value to things in our world that have great value (e.g., other people, other ideas, and other things), so others can see a pattern of bitterness, anger, resentment, and frustration when they hear profanity from others."
Words of Relationship

**GTL to Use When Talking and Communicating with Parents:**

**A student's use of profanity warrants a call to a parent.**

(Note: This GTL phone conversation provides a template you can modify and send to parents as a letter, email, text message, etc.).

"Hello! My name is…. I'm Jamie's teacher. Is now a good time for us to talk?"
Words of Respect

"I'm calling you to share something that happened at school today. Jamie yelled out profanity and disrupted class."
Words of Accountability

"I have talked with Jamie to get an understanding of his behavior. I asked Jamie to help me understand why he used that type of language. I asked him if he was frustrated or angry or didn't feel well. He didn't really want to talk with me about it today."

Words of Understanding

"So I wanted to reach out and make you aware of his behavior and work together to get to the bottom of what is going on with Jamie."

Words of Understanding

"I've shared with the whole class and discussed why profanity is not allowed at school and why choosing profanity can negatively impact their relationships, life, and future."

Words of Guidance

"We also have school policies to make sure our school is a safe place for everyone, and the school's policy is clear about profanity. (State your school's policy for this type of behavior)."

Words of Accountability

"Before we finish our conversation, I wanted to share that I have enjoyed having Jamie in my class. He is… (share something personal, positive, and specific that you've experienced with Jamie and link it to a positive quality that could help Jamie in his future in high school, college and/or career, and life)."

Words of Encouragement

"At the beginning of the school year at the Parent Open House, we talked about the importance of maintaining a strong relationship and open communication between home and school."

Words of Relationship

"Please let me know if you have any questions at all. My hope is for all our students to feel safe, enjoy school, learn as much as they can every day, and be ready for high school and life (use this with middle school students) or college and/or career and life (use this with high school students)."

Words of Hope

## WHAT DO GREAT TEACHERS SAY WHEN…?

**A Student Yells Out a Verbally Aggressive Outburst and/or Acts Out a Physically Aggressive Outburst. (Scenario 7.5)**

(This scenario is a serious one. Anytime students are verbally aggressive or physically aggressive in your classroom, it is a chaotic, scary, emotionally, and physically charged experience for you and all the middle school or high school students in the classroom. Whether they throw something like a chair, shout out harsh and profane words, or act out more intense or aggressive behaviors, it's physically and emotionally stressful for everyone. Notify your school principal immediately to help you handle the situation. Hopefully, these GTL examples offer guidance and understanding for you during this very stressful experience.)

### GTL Reminders to Self:

*Remember…* Aggressive outbursts can indicate a deeper emotional or physical issue. Be sure to give students a second chance whenever possible while letting them know their behavior was not acceptable.

Words of Grace

*Remember…* When you're setting up your classroom rules and behavior expectations, it's important for you to make all students aware of the school policies and consequences for aggressive outbursts in your classroom before they happen.

Words of Guidance

*Remember…* Rather than harboring ill feelings for a student who made an aggressive outburst in your class, demonstrate grace and dig deep to get to the root of the problem to better understand middle school and high school students' behaviors.

Words of Grace

*Remember…* In some cases of aggressive outbursts, you alone may not be able to solve a student's problem, and you will need the help of the guidance counselor and other support personnel in the school.

Words of Guidance

*Remember…* Wanting to get to the root of the problem to better understand middle school and high school students' behaviors such as aggressive outbursts demonstrates love and care.

Words of Love

*Remember…* Provide middle school and high school students a list of effective strategies they can use to prevent aggressive outbursts before they happen (e.g., go to the teacher immediately to ask for help, go to the back of the room to make the mental and emotional shift back to the lesson, put your head down on your desk and count to 10, or ask to talk with the guidance counselor).

Words of Guidance

**GTL to Share with Students:**

(Speaking individually with the outburst student) "I understand something may have caused you to act that way, but you cannot act that way in our class."

Words of Accountability

(After the incident is over). "Help me understand how you were feeling just now. Were you angry at me or someone? I want to understand."

Words of Understanding

(Shared privately to the student) "Do you need a minute before we talk about what happened? You can go to the back of the room or put your head down before we talk about it."

            Words of Grace

(After the phone call with parents) "I appreciate you being honest with your parents about what happened—that's the first step in getting to the truth of what caused you to act that way. Once we know what caused it, we can learn how to prevent it from happening again."

          Words of Encouragement

(To the whole class) "Thank you for staying calm and for helping me with this situation. Please stay in your seats and work quietly while I call the principal."

           Words of Guidance

(To the whole class) "When you are feeling upset or angry and want to act out—Stop—and think about what you can do instead. You can come to me immediately and we can talk, you can go to the back of the room, you can put your head down and count to 10, or you can ask to go and talk with the guidance counselor."

           Words of Guidance

"I'm glad we worked together and came up with a plan for improving your behavior. I know it's going to work because you are a very determined person and when you give your attention to something—you get it done!"

          Words of Encouragement

**GTL to Use When Talking and Communicating with Parents:**

**Phone call to discuss a student's behavior in the classroom: A student makes a verbally aggressive outburst and/or a physically aggressive outburst.**

(This phone call is coming from the principal's office. The principal and the teacher agree that the teacher will lead the phone conversation.)

"Hello! My name is…. I'm Jamie's teacher. Is now a good time for us to talk?"
Words of Respect

"I'm calling to share something that happened in class today. Jamie yelled out and (share the specific verbally and/or physically aggressive behavior)."
Words of Accountability

"I talked with Jamie to get an understanding of his behavior. I asked him to help me understand why he yelled out and (share the specific verbally and/or physically aggressive behavior). I asked him if he was frustrated or angry or didn't feel well."
Words of Understanding

"I have Jamie here in the principal's office with me. He's going to talk with you about what happened."
Words of Accountability

(Jamie tells his parents what happened and is truthful.)

"We have school policies to make sure our school is a safe place for everyone, and the school's policy is clear about the consequences for this type of behavior. (State your school's policy for this type of behavior)."
Words of Accountability

"I want to get to the root of Jamie's behavior and for him to know that I'm not upset with him; however, his behavior was not acceptable—we can't accept this in our class."
Words of Understanding

"So I wanted to reach out and make you aware of his behavior and work together to get to the bottom of what is going on with Jamie. Has Jamie shared anything with you about our class, or other students in our class, that could give us a better understanding of how he's feeling about school?"

Words of Understanding

"Before we finish our conversation, I wanted to share that I have enjoyed having Jamie in my class. He is… (share something personal, positive, and specific that you've experienced with Jamie and link it to a positive quality that could help Jamie in his future in high school, college and/or career, and life)."

Words of Encouragement

"At the beginning of the school year at the Parent Open House, you and I talked about the importance of maintaining a strong relationship and open communication between home and school."

Words of Relationship

"Please let me know if you have any questions at all. My hope is for all our students to feel safe, enjoy school, learn as much as they can every day, and be ready for high school and life (use this with middle school students) or college and/or career and life (use this with high school students)."

Words of Hope

## GTL Classroom Activities to Transform Middle School and High School Student Behavior and Your Classroom Culture

### GTL Classroom Activities for Student Outbursts in Middle School and High School

We see these activities as either "in the moment" or a time to pull your students together for classroom conversations to encourage student voice and student engagement in your classroom.

We see the teacher as a facilitator and co-learner during these GTL activities and students as active participants in learning how to "see the classroom through the lens of the teacher" and how to manage their own current behavior for success and their future behavior as they get ready for high school, college and/ or a career.

1. (Role-Play GTL Scenario for Students to Help Them Practice How to Respectfully Respond to Another Student Who Has an Outburst in Class, such as yelling out, "This is so boring!" or "I'm lost! I don't understand!" or "Why do we have to do this…? When are we ever going to need this or use this?"). Select one student to role-play a student and another student to role-play a student who has an outburst and distracts students from the lesson. Ask the role-playing student who is going to have the outburst to decide which outburst behavior they are going to demonstrate. Allow time for the role-playing student to try to respectfully respond to the outburst student. After the first role-play, ask the role-playing student who had the outburst if what the role-playing student said was helpful and respectful. Encourage the other students in the class to help the role-playing student with what to say and how to respectfully respond to the role-playing student who has the outburst. Continue the role-play activity with new role-players and use the other student outburst scenarios. Conclude each role-playing activity with a discussion of how you, as the teacher, will respectfully respond to students who have outbursts in your classroom.

2. (Hit the Pause Button for Discussion on Student Behavior Expectations Related to Inappropriate Outbursts When Students Yell, "Why Do We Have to Learn This?") Share with the students that you are going to "Hit the Pause Button" on the lesson and take important time to discuss WHY we need to learn this information, why it's relevant to them, and how to respectfully share their frustrations about a lesson. Ask the whole class for their personal

answers for WHY they think this lesson is important and relevant and how they might use it in the future for high school, college and/or career, and life—"Why do you think we need to learn this?" Allow time for students to answer your questions and to share their additional questions and concerns about why the lesson is important. Remind students to come to you quietly and privately if they don't understand the purpose or relevance of the lesson. Conclude the discussion by adding your personal reasons for WHY this lesson is important and relevant to their future in high school, college and/or career, and life.

3. (Getting Ready for Life Discussion about Using Profanity and Making Great Choices) Share with the students that you're about to have a Getting Ready for Life Discussion related to using profanity at school and making great choices. Explain to students how your school has policies about using profanity at school and why those policies are important. Share with your students and spend time discussing why profanity is not allowed at school and why choosing profanity can negatively impact their life and future. Share the following four reasons why using profanity might negatively impact their relationships and their future: (1) it is rude, obscene, and disrespectful, and others are offended and feel disrespected hearing it; (2) it is often spoken with anger, aggression, and disrespect, so others are uncomfortable and feel unsafe hearing it; (3) it demonstrates a lack of self-control and self-management, so others are not quick to trust someone using profanity; and (4) it sometimes communicates a lack of value to things in our world that have great value (e.g., other people, other ideas, and other things), so others can see a pattern of bitterness, anger, resentment, and frustration when they hear profanity from others. Then, break the class into small discussion groups. First, ask students to share their thoughts about these negative relational impacts related to using profanity with their small group. Then ask the students to offer additional reasons why using profanity might negatively impact their relationships

and their future. Circulate around the classroom to listen in on the small group discussions. Allow time for students to share their personal success stories for making great choices and choosing not to use profanity. Bring the whole class back together and ask if any of the groups want to share with the whole class. Remind students how their personal success stories might help and encourage other students to choose respectful language. Conclude the discussion by sharing how making great choices and choosing respectful language will set them up for success for high school, college and/or career, and life.

# 8

# What Do Great Teachers Say When a Student Does Not Show Respect for Themselves or Others?

What do you say when your middle school and high school students do not show respect for themselves, their classmates and/or you? This chapter provides teacher-friendly charts with Great Teacher Language (GTL) Reminders to Self, GTL to Share with Students, GTL to Use When Talking and Communicating with Parents, and GTL Classroom Activities specifically related to the following:

**Scenario 8.1:** A Student is Calling Other Students Disrespectful Names and/or Making Fun of Other Students.
**Scenario 8.2:** A Student is Making Inappropriate Gestures Toward Other Students and/or the Teacher.
**Scenario 8.3:** A Student is Verbally Disrespectful to the Teacher.
**Scenario 8.4:** A Student is Interrupting Another Student and/or the Teacher.
**Scenario 8.5:** A Student is Taking Things That Do Not Belong to Him/Her.
**Scenario 8.6:** A Student is Demonstrating a Lack of Self-Respect.

> We know these are not the only disrespectful behaviors that happen in your classroom. These specific scenarios are a starting point for you to develop your GTL for your classroom. For some of our student behavior scenarios, we have included GTL examples for you to use when talking with parents. These GTL examples are templates for phone conversations, emails, or other types of messages to develop strong communication between teachers and parents and to promote understanding, relationships, trust, and collaboration.

Respect has a powerful ripple effect on those around us. When we give respect, we often get respect in return. When we respect middle school and high school students, they feel empowered, valued, and needed. When students feel respected, they are more likely to demonstrate respect for themselves and others. This powerful and respectful ripple effect will positively impact their current success and their future success in high school, college and/or career, and life. Your Language of Practice (LoP) in the form of GTL can create a culture of mutual respect and offer these disrespectful students the accountability, encouragement, grace, guidance, high expectations, hope, love, relationships, respect, understanding, and unity necessary to successfully engage them in the learning.

Teachers and middle school and high school students often jointly create a rule for their classroom that states: Be respectful. But do students know what respect is? Do they know what great examples of respect look like and sound like in your classroom? If left undefined, respect is a concept that can be abstract for students. The meaning of "respect" is often left open for interpretation, and students develop their own understanding of what it means to them. It is important for teachers to offer a clear definition and concrete examples of true respect. (See GTL Classroom Activities at the end of this chapter.)

We believe middle school and high school students show true respect when they choose to demonstrate a proper regard for the dignity of their own character and the character of others.

It reveals an intentional consideration and appreciation of others. It is so important for teachers to use Words of Respect, demonstrate respect toward their students, and highlight examples of student respect when they occur.

Students might not have a clear understanding of what respect is—but they certainly know what disrespect looks like and sounds like! They also know what disrespect feels like. How do you feel and respond when you are disrespected? If we react to disrespect with disrespect, it can cause a cycle of bigger problems. When middle school and high school students are being disrespectful, our language and actions can certainly make things better or worse.

Disrespectful behaviors are like encrypted messages indicating deeper problems. What if we decoded these messages from the student as "It's not because I am a bad student—I'm just struggling, and I need your help. If we could get to the reason for my disrespect and help me eliminate it, I could be a good student." Why do middle school and high school students choose to be disrespectful to others? What are the underlying reasons? Some students show disrespect to others because they themselves are victims of disrespect. Their feelings of powerlessness and helplessness result in outward disrespect as they seek to overpower and control the teacher or other students. Other disrespectful behavior is an indication that the student feels angry, threatened, insecure, or jealous or seeks revenge.

Understanding why students choose disrespect can help us in guiding them to choose respectful behaviors for their current and future success. If we identify the underlying reason for disrespect, we can separate the student from their behavior and work to eliminate the reason for their disrespectful behavior. When we recognize the underlying reason for the outward show of disrespect, it says to students, "I am here to help you now."

What about the middle school and high school students with a lack of self-respect? Are there outward signs that indicate how they feel on the inside? How can we help them? When students feel inadequate, unworthy, or afraid of failure, they may experience a lack of self-respect. This lack of self-respect results in a wide range of behaviors from subtle to extremely obvious. Some students attempt to become invisible, whereas others seek to be the center of attention. Their class participation may be limited or overbearing as they seek to overcompensate for their feelings of inadequacy. When students feel insecure or unworthy, they often choose reactions that show disrespect toward themselves. These self-disrespecting behaviors can negatively impact learning for the student, their relationships, and their future.

Building and maintaining a culture of mutual respect are essential for middle school and high school student safety and success. It begins with teachers who model respect. When students see and hear us being respectful, they begin to understand what respect really looks like and sounds like and how they can show respect for themselves and others. When students and teachers demonstrate respect for one another, the classroom becomes a safe environment for learning and success. Our goal is for students to learn from our example and start demonstrating self-respect and respect for others that will positively impact their learning and success in school and in their future.

We all want respect from others, and when we freely give it, we expect it in return. However, when we show others respect and get disrespect in return, it creates a discouraging situation and a stormy environment. Trust is lost and relationships are damaged. Fostering a culture of mutual respect in your classroom helps to eliminate these stormy situations. The ultimate goal is for middle school and high school students to demonstrate respect intentionally and to make a conscious decision to show consideration and appreciation for other students, their teachers, and others.

### WHAT DO GREAT TEACHERS SAY WHEN...?

**A Student is Calling Other Students Disrespectful Names and/or Making Fun of Other Students. (Scenario 8.1)**

### GTL Reminders to Self:

*Remember*... Respectful actions are contagious.

Words of Hope

*Remember...* Middle school and high school students need to see and hear concrete examples of what respect looks like and sounds like.

Words of Guidance

*Remember...* It's important to discuss with students how you're going to resolve disrespectful language and behaviors quickly and respectfully to prevent bigger issues from happening.

Words of Accountability

*Remember...* Some students show disrespect to others and make fun of other students because they have been made fun of by someone else.

Words of Understanding

*Remember...* When students feel respected, they are more likely to demonstrate respect for themselves and others.

Words of Encouragement

*Remember...* Some disrespectful behavior is an indication that the student feels angry, threatened, insecure, or jealous or seeks revenge.

Words of Understanding

*Remember...* Modeling respectful language and actions will demonstrate to students how to show respect to others.

Words of Respect

*Remember...* The powerful and respectful ripple effect of demonstrating respect to others will positively impact students' current success and their future success in high school, college and/or career, and life.

Words of Hope

**GTL to Share with Students:**

(Shared with the whole class) "We're going to resolve disrespectful language and behaviors quickly and respectfully to prevent bigger issues from happening."
Words of Accountability

(Shared with the whole class) "When your friends are making fun of somebody, it can be tough to do the right thing and not follow along. I trust that you will make the right decision and show respect to everyone."
Words of Accountability

(Whispering to student) "How would you feel if someone said that to you? How do you feel when someone disrespects you?"
Words of Understanding

"Today, I want us to discuss the importance of respect. Why is it important to show respect for each other? How can showing respect impact your success now and in your future?"
Words of Understanding

"We are all unique! We're all different in our own ways. It's important to respect each other and our differences."
Words of Unity

(Shared with the whole class) "We all have different thoughts and opinions. We want to establish and maintain a culture in our class where no one feels embarrassed to share their thoughts and opinions and everyone feels confident to share."
Words of Unity

"We all make mistakes. At some point, everybody in this class—including me—will do something that causes us to feel embarrassed. Remember what you would feel like if it happened to you, so let's be respectful when this happens and not make it worse for them."

Words of Grace

"When someone does something to hurt your feelings, it is important to talk with them. Once you have discussed it with them and they have apologized—let's agree to forgive and forget."

Words of Grace

**GTL to Use When Talking and Communicating with Parents:**

**Phone call to discuss a student's behavior in the classroom: A student is calling other students disrespectful names and/or making fun of other students, which distracts from the lesson and is causing the other students to be angry and frustrated.**

(Note: This GTL phone conversation provides a template you can modify and send to parents as a letter, email, text message, etc.).

"Hello! My name is…. I'm Jamie's teacher. He's not in trouble. Is now a good time for us to talk?"

Words of Respect

"I enjoy having Jamie in my class. He is… (share something personal, positive, and specific that you've experienced with Jamie and link it to a positive quality that could help Jamie in his future in high school, college and/or career, and life)."

Words of Encouragement

"Since the first day of school, we have been talking about respectful behaviors in our class and the

importance of showing respect to one another. We've also discussed how we're going to resolve disrespectful language and behaviors quickly and respectfully to prevent bigger issues from happening."
Words of Accountability

"I'm calling you to share something that happened today. Jamie was calling other students disrespectful names and making fun of them during class."
Words of Accountability

"I talked with Jamie to get an understanding about his behavior. I also asked Jamie if other students have been calling him disrespectful names or making fun of him. He told me that no one was calling him disrespectful names or making fun of him. We don't want anybody to feel disrespected at school."
Words of Understanding

"I wanted to mention this to you and let you know about this issue. I encouraged Jamie to apologize to the other students. I am so proud of Jamie because he did apologize, and he and the other students were able to continue working on the project together."
Words of Unity

"Please let me know if you have any questions at all. My hope is for all our students to feel safe, enjoy school, learn as much as they can every day, and be ready for high school and life (use this with middle school students) or college and/or career and life (use this with high school students)."
Words of Hope

## WHAT DO GREAT TEACHERS SAY WHEN...?

**A Student is Making Inappropriate Gestures Toward Other Students and/or the Teacher. (Scenario 8.2)**

### GTL Reminders to Self:

*Remember...* When you take student disrespect personally, you can lose sight of a possible solution to solve a bigger problem.

Words of Understanding

*Remember...* When you model respect, it can change your middle school and high school students' way of thinking and acting.

Words of Guidance

*Remember...* If you don't hold students accountable in the moment, it can lead to a classroom environment where students become accustomed to constant meaningless reminders, fail to see their impact on others, and start to do what they want to do.

Words of Accountability

*Remember...* When middle school and high school students make inappropriate gestures toward you, it is important for you to provide a respectful response that creates an accountable and safe environment and shows the student that you care about them.

Words of Love

*Remember...* When students and teachers demonstrate respect for one another, the classroom becomes a safe environment for learning and success.

Words of Encouragement

*Remember...* Encourage your students to treat other students the way they want to be treated.

Words of High Expectations

*Remember…* Inappropriate gestures can indicate a deeper emotional or physical issue. Be sure to give students a second chance whenever possible while letting them know their behavior was not acceptable.

Words of Grace

*Remember…* Rather than harboring ill feelings for a student who makes an inappropriate gesture toward other students or you, demonstrate grace and dig deep to get to the root of the problem to better understand middle school and high school students' behaviors.

Words of Grace

### GTL to Share with Students:

(Speaking individually with the student) "I understand something may have caused you to act that way, but you cannot act that way in our class."

Words of Accountability

(Privately to the student) "Help me understand how you were feeling just now. Were you angry at me or someone? I want to understand."

Words of Understanding

"I care about you, so I am going to hold you accountable for the choices you make."

Words of Love

(Whispering to the student) "Right now, you might not like me as your teacher, but I do deserve your respect, and I am going to respect you."

Words of Respect

(Shared with the whole class after a class game) "Whether you win or lose, let's agree to be supportive of each other and congratulate the winners. Good character and sportsmanship show we are able to win with character and lose with dignity."

Words of Encouragement

(Shared with the whole class) "Let's discuss how to respect each other. What does it look like and sound like when we show respect for someone?"
Word of Understanding

"That was very unkind and disrespectful. How could you have handled that differently?"
Words of Accountability

"Even when you're disrespectful and you misbehave, I want to help you. I want you to be successful—so let's figure out a way for that to happen."
Words of Grace

### GTL to Use When Talking and Communicating with Parents:

**Phone call to discuss a student's behavior in the classroom: A student is making inappropriate gestures at other students and/or the teacher.**

(Note: This GTL phone conversation provides a template you can modify and send to parents as a letter, email, text message, etc.).

"Hello! My name is…. I'm Jamie's teacher. Is now a good time for us to talk?"
Words of Respect

"I'm calling you to share something that happened today at school. Jamie made an inappropriate gesture toward me in class." (State the specific inappropriate behavior.)
Words of Accountability

"I talked with Jamie to get an understanding about his behavior. I wanted him to know that I'm not upset with him; however, his behavior was not acceptable."
Words of Understanding

"So I wanted to reach out and make you aware of his behavior and work together to get to the bottom of what is going on with Jamie. Has Jamie shared anything with you about me, or about our class, that could give us a better understanding of how he's feeling about school?"
Words of Understanding

"We have school policies to make sure our school is a safe place for everyone, and the school's policy is clear about inappropriate gestures." (State your school's policy for this type of behavior.)
Words of Accountability

"Since the first day of school, we have been talking about respectful behaviors in our class and the importance of showing respect to one another. We've also discussed how we're going to resolve disrespectful language and behaviors quickly and respectfully to prevent bigger issues from happening."
Words of Accountability

"Before we finish our conversation, I wanted to share that I have enjoyed having Jamie in my class. He is… (share something personal, positive, and specific that you've experienced with Jamie and link it to a positive quality that could help Jamie in his future in high school, college and/or career, and life)."
Words of Encouragement

"At the beginning of the school year at the Parent Open House, we talked about the importance of maintaining a strong relationship and open communication between home and school."
Words of Relationship

"Please let me know if you have any questions at all. My hope is for all our students to feel safe, enjoy

school, learn as much as they can every day, and be ready for high school and life (use this with middle school students) or college and/or career and life (use this with high school students)."

Words of Hope

## WHAT DO GREAT TEACHERS SAY WHEN...?

**A Student is Verbally Disrespectful to the Teacher. (Scenario 8.3)**

### GTL Reminders to Self:

*Remember...* Don't allow disrespectful student behavior to become a personal conflict—you vs. student. Keep the focus on helping the student and not on defending yourself or maintaining power, saving face, and so on.

Words of Unity

*Remember...* When students see and hear us being respectful, they begin to understand what respect really looks like and sounds like and how they can show respect for themselves and others.

Words of Respect

*Remember...* It's rare for middle school and high school students to hear an authority figure say "I'm sorry" or "I made a mistake." This honest and transparent language teaches them that an apology can restore a relationship now and relationships in their future.

Words of Relationship

*Remember...* When we are dealing with disrespectful behaviors, students need to see and hear a consistency in our actions and our language.

Words of Accountability

*Remember…* When middle school and high school students are verbally disrespectful to you, it is important for you to provide a respectful response that creates an accountable and safe environment and shows the student that you care about them.

Words of Love

*Remember…* Respect has a powerful ripple effect on those around us. When we give respect, we often get respect in return.

Words of Encouragement

*Remember…* Verbally disrespectful language can indicate a deeper emotional or physical issue. Be sure to give students a second chance whenever possible while letting them know their behavior was not acceptable.

Words of Grace

*Remember…* Rather than harboring ill feelings for a student who is verbally disrespectful to you, demonstrate grace and dig deep to get to the root of the problem to better understand middle school and high school students' behaviors.

Words of Grace

### GTL to Share with Students:

(Speaking individually with the student) "I understand something may have caused you to speak that way, but you cannot talk that way in our class."

Words of Accountability

(Privately to the verbally disrespectful student) "Help me understand how you were feeling just now. Were you angry at me or someone? I want to understand."

Words of Understanding

"We are not always going to agree, but when we have disagreements, we owe each other respect."
                                    Words of Respect

"When I disagree with you, I'm going to do my best to model for you what it sounds like to respectfully disagree with someone."
                                    Words of Guidance

"Everybody in our classroom is different and we will not always agree with each other, but everyone deserves our respect and kindness."
                                    Words of Unity

"I understand what you are saying, but I don't agree with it. Let's agree to disagree and keep the conversation going."
                                    Word of Respect

(Whispering to a verbally disrespectful student) "I don't like it when you talk to me that way and disrespect me, but I still care about you."
                                    Words of Grace

"We really need to watch what we say. Words do matter."
                                    Words of Respect

"As a class, let's discuss what respect sounds like. What does it sound like when we show respect for someone?"
                                    Words of Guidance

**GTL to Use When Talking and Communicating with Parents:**

**Phone call to discuss a student's behavior in the classroom: A student is verbally disrespectful to you.**
   (Note: This GTL phone conversation provides a template you can modify and send to parents as a letter, email, text

message, and so on. You will notice that this GTL phone call conversation is very similar to the previous GTL phone call when *a student is making inappropriate gestures toward other students and/or the teacher*. We hope the GTL similarities will provide you with a GTL framework and a working template for future phone calls with parents to maintain a strong relationship and open communication between home and school.)

"Hello! My name is…. I'm Jamie's teacher. Is now a good time for us to talk?"
Words of Respect

"I'm calling you to share something that happened today at school. Jamie was verbally disrespectful to me in class." (State the specific inappropriate behavior.)
Words of Accountability

"I talked with Jamie to get an understanding about his behavior. I wanted him to know that I'm not upset with him; however, his language was not acceptable."
Words of Understanding

"So I wanted to reach out and make you aware of his behavior and work together to get to the bottom of what is going on with Jamie. Has Jamie shared anything with you about me, or about our class, that could give us a better understanding of how he's feeling about school?"
Words of Understanding

"We have school policies to make sure our school is a safe place for everyone, and the school's policy is clear about a student's verbal disrespect to teachers." (State your school's policy for this type of behavior.)
Words of Accountability

"Since the first day of school, we have been talking about respectful behaviors in our class and the

importance of showing respect to one another. We've also discussed how we're going to resolve disrespectful language and behaviors quickly and respectfully to prevent bigger issues from happening."
Words of Accountability

"Before we finish our conversation, I wanted to share that I have enjoyed having Jamie in my class. He is… (share something personal, positive, and specific that you've experienced with Jamie and link it to a positive quality that could help Jamie in his future in high school, college and/or career, and life)."
Words of Encouragement

"At the beginning of the school year at the Parent Open House, we talked about the importance of maintaining a strong relationship and open communication between home and school."
Words of Relationship

"Please let me know if you have any questions at all. My hope is for all our students to feel safe, enjoy school, learn as much as they can every day, and be ready for high school and life (use this with middle school students) or college and/or career and life (use this with high school students)."
Words of Hope

## WHAT DO GREAT TEACHERS SAY WHEN…?

**A Student is Interrupting Another Student and/or the Teacher. (Scenario 8.4)**

### GTL Reminders to Self:

*Remember…* Building and maintaining a culture of mutual respect begin with teachers who model respect.
Words of Guidance

*Remember…* It's difficult to get respect without being willing to give it.

Words of Respect

*Remember…* Some students show disrespect to others because they themselves are victims of disrespect.

Words of Understanding

*Remember…* By talking with students respectfully, they can get the sense of "Maybe this teacher cares."

Words of Love

*Remember…* Love and respect for students in spite of what they do is grace in action.

Words of Grace

*Remember…* Sometimes students interrupt others because they are excited to share their thoughts and ideas.

Words of Encouragement

### GTL to Share with Students:

(Speaking individually with the student) "I understand something may have caused you to interrupt our class that way, but you cannot interrupt that way in our class."

Words of Accountability

(Privately to the student) "Help me understand how you were feeling just now. I want to understand why you interrupted our lesson."

Words of Understanding

(Share with the whole class) "I am responsible for making sure all of you have the chance to learn and the chance to complete your assignments without interruptions."

Words of High Expectations

"Please watch yourself and do not interrupt or distract others while they're working on assignments."
Words of Guidance

"Let's agree to hold ourselves accountable and show each other respect in our class."
Words of Accountability

"I really want to hear everyone's thoughts about today's topic. Let's remember to listen to everyone and give them our full attention."
Words of Unity

(Privately to student) "I appreciate how you waited to speak and gave the other students your attention while they were speaking. That was very respectful."
Words of Encouragement

"It is so important to respect others by listening when they are speaking in class."
Words of Respect

"If someone interrupts the lesson in our classroom, it is important to think about how you will respectfully react to that interruption."
Words of Understanding

(To the whole class) "Thank you for staying focused on our lesson and not allowing the interruption to become a bigger distraction."
Words of Guidance

## WHAT DO GREAT TEACHERS SAY WHEN...?

**A Student is Taking Things That Do Not Belong to Him/Her. (Scenario 8.5)**

### GTL Reminders to Self:

*Remember...* Middle school and high school students have lots of different reasons for taking things that do not belong to them. They might take food because they are hungry, they might take class supplies because they don't have them, they take things because they want what they don't have, and sometimes they take things for a deeper reason.

Words of Understanding

*Remember...* Students who need class supplies may be embarrassed to share that need with you.

Words of Relationship

*Remember...* Your students are watching how you model respect for other teachers, parents, students, and the principal. What you "say and do" can be a great model of the respect you expect to see from them.

Words of High Expectations

*Remember...* Students make some inappropriate choices at times and will need to be redirected.

Words of Grace

*Remember...* Establishing mutual respect within your class will help your students to respect each other's belongings.

Words of Unity

*Remember...* Encourage students to share with you when they have needs, like class supplies, pencils, paper, food, and so on.

Words of Love

*Remember…* When students take things that don't belong to them, it can indicate a deeper emotional or physical issue. Be sure to give students a second chance whenever possible while letting them know their behavior was not acceptable.
Words of Grace

*Remember…* Demonstrate grace and dig deep to get to the root of the problem to better understand middle school and high school students' behaviors when they take things that don't belong to them.
Words of Grace

### GTL to Share with Students:

(Speaking individually with the student) "I understand something may have caused you to take that item from the other student, but you cannot take something that doesn't belong to you."
Words of Accountability

(Privately to the student) "Help me understand what you need and why you took that item."
Words of Understanding

"It's so important to respect other students' belongings. If you would like to see it or use it, you'll need to ask their permission."
Words of Respect

"If you need something you don't have, before you take something that does not belong to you, please remember to ask me if I can help you."
Words of Love

(Shared with the whole class) "We have school policies to make sure our school is a safe place for everyone, and the school's policy is clear about taking things that

belong to other students." (Share your school's policy for this type of behavior.)
Words of Accountability

"To maintain a culture of mutual respect, I'm going to encourage each of you to understand the importance of respecting other people's belongings."
Words of Encouragement

(Shared with the whole class) "In our class, we want to be able to trust one another. I'm going to be honest with you, and I hope you will all be honest with me. If you take something that doesn't belong to you, it's important to take personal responsibility and return the item. That's an act of integrity and will help restore trust with others now and in the future."
Words of Relationship

"I really appreciate your honesty. When you are honest with me it shows me you respect yourself enough to tell the truth."
Words of Encouragement

**GTL to Use When Talking and Communicating with Parents:**

**Phone call to discuss a student's behavior in the classroom: A student is taking things that do not belong to him/her.**

(Note: This GTL phone conversation provides a template you can modify and send to parents as a letter, email, text message, etc.).

"Hello! My name is…. I'm Jamie's teacher. Is now a good time for us to talk?"
Words of Respect

"I'm calling you to share something that happened today at school. A student came to me and said that Jamie took something from him that did not belong to Jamie."
Words of Accountability

"I talked with Jamie to find out what exactly was going on and to get his side of the story."
Words of Understanding

"Jamie admitted he took the item from the other student. I was proud of Jamie's honesty."
Words of Encouragement

"We are reminding students it's so important to respect other students' belongings, and if they would like to see or use something that doesn't belong to them, they need to ask for permission. Our goal is to promote mutual respect in our class."
Words of Guidance

"We have school policies to make sure our school is a safe place for everyone, and the school's policy is clear about taking things that belong to other students." (Share your school's policy for this type of behavior.)
Words of Accountability

"I wanted you to know I encourage students to let me know when they need something they might have forgotten at home that day, like pencils, paper, a snack, and other things they might need."
Words of Love

"Before we finish our conversation, I wanted to share that I have enjoyed having Jamie in my class. He is… (share something personal, positive, and specific that you've experienced with Jamie and link it to a positive quality that could help Jamie in his future in high school, college and/or career, and life)."
Words of Encouragement

"Please let me know if you have any questions at all. My hope is for all our students to feel safe, enjoy

school, learn as much as they can every day, and be ready for high school and life (use this with middle school students) or college and/or career and life (use this with high school students)."

Words of Hope

## WHAT DO GREAT TEACHERS SAY WHEN…?

**A Student is Demonstrating a Lack of Self-Respect. (Scenario 8.6)**

### GTL Reminders to Self:

*Remember…* Talking individually with middle school and high school students gives us greater insight into their life, their thoughts, and their needs.

Words of Relationship

*Remember…* Students need a teacher who wants the best for them and who is looking out for them and guiding them in genuine love all along the way.

Words of Love

*Remember…* When students feel inadequate, unworthy, or afraid of failure, they may experience a lack of self-respect. This lack of self-respect results in a wide range of behaviors from subtle to extremely obvious.

Words of Understanding

*Remember…* When students are demonstrating a lack of personal respect, their class participation may be limited or overbearing as they seek to overcompensate for their feelings of inadequacy and insecurity.

Words of Guidance

*Remember…* Self-disrespecting behaviors can negatively impact learning for students.

Words of Understanding

*Remember…* When students have low self-respect, look for their positive behaviors to celebrate.
Words of High Expectations

*Remember…* When students have low self-respect, it can indicate a deeper emotional or physical issue. Give these students attention and encourage them to talk to you or someone they trust about how they're feeling.
Words of Grace

*Remember…* Demonstrate grace and dig deep to get to the root of the problem to better understand middle school and high school students' behaviors when they demonstrate low self-respect.
Words of Grace

### GTL to Share with Students:

(Speaking individually with the student) "It seems like you're being too hard on yourself about this issue. Do you want to talk about what's going on?"
Words of Accountability

(Privately to the student) "Help me understand what you need and how I can help you?"
Words of Understanding

(When you want to help a student shift from a mindset of a lack of self-respect to one of self-respect. You can personalize this GTL for the specific student.) "I've noticed you're really good at art. I could use your help with this new bulletin board. Could you help me think about how to design it?"
Words of Understanding

"I believe in you. Even though you might not think you can do this, I believe you can."
Words of Love

(When students have low self-respect, look for positive behaviors to celebrate. You can personalize this GTL for the specific student.) "I really appreciate and respect how you have helped make our new student feel welcomed this week."
Words of Encouragement

(Whispering to student with low self-respect about a low grade) "You're going to be OK. Don't be so hard on yourself. I know you can do better and I'm going to work with you."
Words of Grace

"If you don't respect yourself, then it's almost impossible for you to respect others."
Words of Respect

**GTL to Use When Talking and Communicating with Parents:**

**Phone call to discuss a student's behavior in the classroom: A student is demonstrating a lack of self-respect—a student is being too hard on himself.**

(Note: This GTL phone conversation provides a template you can modify and send to parents as a letter, email, text message, etc.).

"Hello! My name is…. I'm Jamie's teacher. He's not in trouble. Is now a good time for us to talk?"
Words of Respect

"I enjoy having Jamie in my class. He is… (share something personal, positive, and specific that you've experienced with Jamie and link it to a positive quality that could help Jamie in his future in high school, college and/or career, and life)."
Words of Encouragement

"I'm calling you to share something I noticed today at school. Jamie was really hard on himself when we were working on a class project. He said multiple times that "I can't do this, I'm an idiot."
Words of Accountability

"I talked with Jamie to get an understanding about his behavior. I wanted him to know that I think he is very capable of doing the work and that I'm here to help him when it gets challenging."
Words of Understanding

"In our class, our goal is to promote mutual respect. We talk about the importance of self-respect and respecting others, and I wanted to reach out and make you aware of his behavior and work together to get to the bottom of what is going on with Jamie."
Words of Understanding

"Has Jamie shared anything with you about me, or about our class, that could give us a better understanding of how he's feeling about school?"
Words of Understanding

"At the beginning of the school year at the Parent Open House, we talked about the importance of maintaining a strong relationship and open communication between home and school."
Words of Relationship

"Please let me know if you have any questions at all. My hope is for all our students to feel safe, enjoy school, learn as much as they can every day, and be ready for high school and life (use this with middle school students) or college and/or career and life (use this with high school students)."
Words of Hope

## GTL Classroom Activities to Transform Middle School and High School Student Behavior and Your Classroom Culture

### GTL Classroom Activities for Middle School and High School Students Who Do Not Show Respect for Themselves and Others

We see these activities as either "in the moment" or a time to pull your students together for classroom conversations to encourage student voice and student engagement in your classroom.

We see the teacher as a facilitator and co-learner during these GTL activities and students as active participants in learning how to "see the classroom through the lens of the teacher" and how to manage their own current behavior for success and their future behavior as they get ready for high school, college and/or a career.

1. (Role-Play GTL Scenario for Students Who are Demonstrating a Lack of Self-Respect and Being Hard on Themselves) Select one student to role-play a teacher and one student to role-play a student who is demonstrating a lack of self-respect and being hard on himself/herself. Allow time for the student to role-play his/her lack of self-respect by saying things like "I can't do this, I'm an idiot." Allow time for the role-playing teacher to share encouraging and respectful words with the student. After the role-play, ask the self-disrespecting student if what the role-playing teacher said was helpful. Encourage the other students in the class to help the role-playing teacher with what to say and how to respectfully respond to the student to help them shift from a lack of self-respect to self-respect. In addition, ask the other students in the class to share specific strengths and positive qualities they see in the self-disrespecting role-playing student. Conclude the role-playing activity with a discussion of how you, as the teacher, can respectfully help students shift from a lack of self-respect to self-respect.
2. (Hit the Pause Button for Discussion on Student Behavior Expectations Related to Recognizing and Celebrating

Mutual Respect in the Classroom When You See Multiple Students *Being Respectful*) Share with the students that you are going to "Hit the Pause Button" on the lesson and take important time to share with the students the respectful behavior you saw and the respectful language you heard from students today and you're going to celebrate it. Share the specific examples of the respectful behavior and language you saw and heard and give those students some type of cool reward (e.g., class pride points, school pride points, or school bucks if you have an incentive program). Ask students to think about examples of respectful behavior and respectful language they could use with others to promote respect and school pride. Allow time for each student to share one of their examples. Conclude the discussion by sharing how you will continue to watch and listen for respectful behaviors that promote high levels of mutual respect and school pride.

3. (Getting Ready for Life Discussion about Respecting Others When They Disrespect You and Making Great Choices) Share with the students that you're about to have a Getting Ready for Life discussion related to respecting others when they disrespect you and making great choices. Share your personal experiences of when you chose to show disrespect when someone showed you disrespect. Then, share your success stories when you chose to show respect when someone was disrespectful to you. Allow time for students to share their personal success stories for making great choices and choosing to show respect to people who have disrespected them. Remind students how their personal success stories might help and encourage other students to choose to be respectful to others when others are disrespectful to them. Conclude the discussion by sharing how making great choices and choosing to be respectful when others are disrespectful to them will set them up for success for high school, college and/or career, and life.

# 9

# What Do Great Teachers Say When a Student Refuses to Cooperate or Challenges Them?

What do you say when a middle school or a high school student refuses to cooperate or challenges you (e.g., questions your decisions, questions your authority, refuses to do work, confronts you in front of the class, or demonstrates blatant disrespect). This chapter provides teacher-friendly charts with Great Teacher Language (GTL) Reminders to Self, GTL to Share with Students, GTL to Use When Talking and Communicating with Parents, and GTL Classroom Activities specifically related to the following:

Scenario 9.1: A Student Consistently Asks Questions that Challenge You and/or the Lesson You Are Teaching.
Scenario 9.2: A Student Disagrees With You and Says, "You're Wrong! That's Not What We Were Taught Before!"
Scenario 9.3: A Student Refuses to Cooperate with You and Says, "You're Not My Mom! You Can't Tell Me What To Do! You Can't Make Me Do This Work!"
Scenario 9.4: A Student is Outwardly Angry and Blatantly Disrespectful Toward You.

> We know these are not the only uncooperative or challenging behaviors that happen in your classroom. These specific scenarios are a starting point for you to develop your GTL for your classroom. For some of our student behavior scenarios, we have included GTL examples for you to use when talking with parents. These GTL examples are templates for phone conversations, emails, or other types of messages to develop strong communication between teachers and parents and to promote understanding, relationships, trust and collaboration.

When middle school and high school students refuse to cooperate and challenge us in the classroom, it is important to get to the root of the problem and ask ourselves:

- Is this student frustrated with me, or is the student trying to make sense of the material?
- Or is this student's disagreeable behavior toward me their way of sharing their own opinion?
- Or is this student feeling threatened in some way and setting up a power struggle with me?
- Or is this the student's way of telling me they are angry about something?

Our GTL goal is to help uncooperative and challenging middle school and high school students experience a learning environment that supports and encourages (1) critical thinking, (2) mutual respect where all students feel free to share their own opinions respectfully, (3) win-win relational outcomes between the teacher and students, and (4) students to develop personal strategies to defuse their anger or defiance before it impacts their learning. Your Language of Practice (LoP) in the form of GTL can offer these uncooperative or challenging students the accountability, encouragement, grace, guidance, high expectations, hope, love, relationships, respect, understanding, and unity they need in the moment and beyond. The following section provides relevant and helpful background information for the four scenarios in this chapter.

*Scenario 9.1: A student consistently asks questions that challenge you and/or the lesson you are teaching.*

When middle school and high school students are asking so many questions about the lesson, and their questioning seems rude or arrogant, we can feel challenged and may get defensive. When their critical thinking and questioning are disrespectful, it is important to hold these students accountable for their disrespectful behaviors. As we work with these critical thinkers and prepare them for success in high school, college and/or career, and life, we need to approach them carefully to ensure their respect for us and our respect for their curiosity. When they question why they need to learn the material, we need to be ready to tell them why. When they ask questions over and over, we need to help them make sense of what they are learning. We also need to answer them honestly if we do not know the answer to their questions: "I don't know, but let's find out together." As we work toward our GTL goal to encourage critical thinking and critical thinkers, the students need to see that we are learners, too. These questions can be an opportunity for us to say, "That's a great question—I've never thought about it that way."

*Scenario 9.2: A student disagrees with you and says, "You're wrong! That's not what we were taught before!"*

A GTL goal for your classroom is to promote open and honest classroom discussions where middle school and high school students can develop and share their own opinions. As students feel the freedom to share their opinions, some students might feel the freedom to disrespectfully disagree with you in front of the class. When students share their opinions disrespectfully or are being disrespectfully disagreeable with you, it is important to hold them accountable for their disrespect, redirect them back to the lesson, and remind them of the class expectation of showing mutual respect. Mutual respect is shown when we value everyone as a person, show respect for everyone's opinion, and share our own opinion respectfully. As we work with disrespectfully opinionated and disagreeable students, it is important to address their disrespectful opinions and disagreeable attitudes, while we value their input and be ready to help them see other points of view. When students say they weren't taught something a specific way before, we can be curious to learn how they were taught the information in the past. These disagreements can be an opportunity for us to say,

> "That's an interesting way to think about it—I've never thought about it that way. I don't agree with you, but in order for us to move ahead in our lesson, we need to agree to disagree for now. Let's talk about how you learned that information in the past. I respect you and want to hear more about your opinion—let's talk more after class."

*Scenario 9.3: A student refuses to cooperate with you and says, "You're not my mom! You can't tell me what to do! You can't make me do this work!"*

Have you ever heard these words? What did you say? What did you want to say? It is usually our inclination to fight power with power, especially when we are the authority in the classroom. However, we believe it is important to always avoid a power struggle with a student. Giving back to students what they give you and trying to overpower them creates a lose-lose situation and can derail learning in the classroom.

Coercion might seem to work in the short term; however, for long-term change—real change and real relationships—we propose you adopt a more persuasive stance that says to middle school and high school students, "You are right. I can't make you do it—I can't make you do anything. It's not my job to make you do an assignment; it's my job to teach you and help you in any way I can. The choice is up to you." It is important for students to understand that the choice to cooperate is up to them and that they will be held accountable for their choices. If they do not complete an assignment or refuse to cooperate, there are consequences. If they do complete the assignment or choose to cooperate, there are different consequences. The choice is up to them. It is our responsibility to help them work through these consequences—good or bad—and learn from them. Our GTL goal is to help students become self-managed where they are empowered to make better choices for themselves and experience better consequences too.

This persuasive stance places the focus back on the students' freedom to choose their own behaviors and holds students accountable for their choices. So, if power struggles with students are a "lose-lose" proposition, then how do we get to a "win-win"? How do we prevent a "lose-lose" situation when students challenge us? If we use coercion to deal with the issue, then students can feel threatened, backed into a corner, ready for competition, and *not* ready for learning. They feel that decisions are being made for them, and they don't have a choice in the matter—they lose and we lose. If we ignore challenging and uncooperative students, then they continue with their poor choices without proper guidance—another lose-lose.

What does a "win-win" solution look like and sound like when a student is challenging and uncooperative? It is important to show and tell students that our goal is not to win the power struggle against them. Our GTL goal is to show them we are on the same team—and our ultimate goal is their success! We experience success when our students find success. We believe a "win-win" solution occurs when we demonstrate to students that our intention is not "to work and fight against them" but rather to "work and fight for them." A "win-win" solution becomes more likely when students know we are on their side, we understand and validate their feelings, and we will work with them to find a solution that will help them now and for their future.

*Scenario 9.4: A student is outwardly angry and blatantly disrespectful toward you.*

People get angry. It's unrealistic to think that everyone is going to be happy every day in our classroom. We can't stop middle school and high school students from being angry and disrespectful, but we can help students learn how to work through their anger and defiance to develop self-management. Without self-management, students act out their anger and defiance in the classroom and negatively impact the learning environment. It is important for teachers to get to know their students and build trusting relationships that will lead to personal conversations about the causes of their anger and defiance. When a student shares their anger and defiance triggers with the teacher, this honest realization is one of the first steps toward self-management. Then, the teacher and student together can develop personal self-management strategies to stop the anger and defiance before they start. Self-management also prevents anger and defiance from escalating into more verbally and physically aggressive student behaviors.

When middle school and high school students come to school with anger and defiance already overwhelming them, or they become angry at school, we can see it in their faces and hear it in the tone of their voices. Often their anger and defiance lead to behaviors and emotions that push teachers further away and perpetuate feelings of isolation and rebellion. These students really need for us to see them fully—and recognize and address both their inappropriate behaviors and their need for our care and support. It is important for our words and actions to convey to students that we are on the lookout for these warning signs—ready to offer grace, guidance, accountability, and hope—and ready to say to them, "I am aware, and I care."

## WHAT DO GREAT TEACHERS SAY WHEN...?

**A Student Consistently Asks Questions that Challenge You and/or the Lesson You Are Teaching. (Scenario 9.1)**

### GTL Reminders to Self:

*Remember…* Grace is a powerful way to show patience and love for middle school and high school students who seem to be challenging you.

Words of Grace

*Remember…* Instead of admonishing students for asking questions that challenge you or the lesson you are teaching, offer them assistance and clearer guidance about how to respectfully ask their questions.

Words of Guidance

*Remember…* When students are asking you challenging questions, it doesn't always mean they are challenging your authority.

Words of Understanding

*Remember…* It's important to promote critical thinking in your classroom. When you are teaching and students are learning, some students may ask challenging questions that derail your lesson plan. As we work with these critical thinkers, we need to approach them carefully to ensure their respect for us and our respect for their curiosity.

Words of Respect

*Remember…* Take time to call parents and let them know when their child is excited about learning and curious about the topic you're teaching. This positive phone call is an excellent way to maintain a strong relationship and open communication between home and school.

Words of Unity

*Remember…* As we work to encourage critical thinking and critical thinkers, our students need to see that we are learners, too.

Words of High Expectations

*Remember…* Some of your students strive to get the right answers before their classmates and see it as a competition they must win.

Words of Guidance

**GTL to Share with Students:**

(Shared with the whole class) "I want us to become life-long learners and curious about learning. So please feel free to respectfully ask questions."

Words of Respect

(Shared with the whole class) "Let's talk about why this lesson is important and how it is impacting our world today."

Words of Unity

(Shared with the whole class) "This information (share something content-specific) is going to help you as you." (Share something specific about the link to their future in high school, college and/or career, or their future.)

Words of Hope

"You're really thinking about this topic in such a great way. It's good because you are challenging me and your classmates to consider other possibilities."

Words of Encouragement

(Privately to student) "You've got some great questions, but you need to work on how to ask them. It's hard to listen to your questions and comments when they are disrespectful. Let's talk about how you can ask the same questions in a different way."

Words of Guidance

"That's a great question—and, honestly, I don't know the answer. Let's work together and try to find the answer."

Words of Unity

"That is one way to think about it. Does anyone else have a different idea".

Words of Respect

"I really love your curiosity about this topic. You've made me want to learn more about it, too."

Words of Love

**GTL to Use When Talking and Communicating with Parents:**

**Positive phone call to celebrate a student's behavior in your classroom: A student is demonstrating great curiosity and excitement about the lesson and asking excellent questions that motivate everyone's learning**.

(Note: This GTL phone conversation provides a template you can modify and send to parents as a letter, email, text message, etc.).

"Hello! My name is…. I'm Jamie's teacher. He's not in trouble. Is now a good time for us to talk?"

Words of Respect

"I'm calling you to share something great I noticed today at school. Jamie has been so excited about what we are learning in Biology this week. He has been asking questions, sharing information he has learned on his own, and motivating other students to learn more, too."

Words of Encouragement

"Jamie has such a natural curiosity about Biology, and he is always so engaged in Biology class. He's a great role model for the other students in our class. I am proud of him and his desire to learn."

Words of Relationship

"I can see Jamie having a job in the field of Biology one day."

Words of High Expectations

"At the beginning of the school year at the Parent Open House, we talked about the importance of maintaining a strong relationship and open communication between home and school. That's why I called today to share the great news about Jamie."

Words of Relationship

"Please let me know if you have any questions at all. My hope is for all our students to feel safe, enjoy school, learn as much as they can every day, and be ready for high school and life (use this with middle school students) or college and/or career and life (use this with high school students)."

Words of Hope

## WHAT DO GREAT TEACHERS SAY WHEN...?

**A Student Disagrees With You and Says, "You're Wrong! That's Not What We Were Taught Before!" (Scenario 9.2)**

### GTL Reminders to Self:

*Remember…* Sometimes middle school and high school students think they can look cool or get an ego boost by challenging authority in front of their peers. Be careful not to get tangled in a war of words. Stay calm, remain professional, and do not allow your emotional buttons to get pushed.

Words of Guidance

*Remember…* Asking a student to consider a different point of view demonstrates respect, and telling a student their point of view is wrong demonstrates disrespect.

Words of Respect

*Remember…* As we work with disrespectfully opinionated and disagreeable students, it is important to hold them accountable for their disrespectful opinions and disagreeable attitudes, while we value their input and be ready to help them see other points of view.
Words of Grace

*Remember…* When students share their opinions disrespectfully or are being disrespectfully disagreeable with you, it is important to hold them accountable for their disrespect, redirect them back to the lesson, and remind them of the class expectation of showing mutual respect.
Words of Accountability

*Remember…* Don't be afraid to share with your students what matters most to you and about who you are (your family, your hobbies, and your interests). Take time to get to know who your students are. Find out what motivates them and what they care about and enjoy. Once they get to know you better and connect with you, they might stop their disrespectful behavior toward you.
Words of Love

*Remember…* Involving parents in your classroom is an excellent way to impact the behavior of your students. When students see their parents involved at school, trusting you and supporting you, their own behavior toward you can improve.
Words of Unity

### GTL to Share with Students:

(Whispering to a student) "That was not the best way to share your disagreement, but that's an interesting perspective. I've never thought about it that way. Let's talk about how you could have shared your disagreement more respectfully."
Words of Accountability

(Whispering to a student) "I understand that you're entitled to your own opinion, and I want you to be able to share it. However, the way you just expressed it to the class was inappropriate. There are so many ways to tell others how you are thinking and feeling without being disrespectful."
Words of Respect

(Shared with the whole class) "I'm going to hold you accountable when you are being disrespectfully disagreeable, and I'm going to redirect you back to the lesson and remind you of the class expectation of showing mutual respect."
Words of Accountability

"I think we have a misunderstanding. Let's discuss it."
Words of Understanding

"Hold on, say that again. I really want to hear what you were saying—let's talk about how you learned that information in the past."
Words of Relationship

"To maintain classroom unity, it's really important that we talk through our disagreements with respect and understanding."
Words of Grace

"That's an interesting way to think about it—I've never thought about it that way. I don't agree with you, but in order for us to move ahead in our lesson, we need to agree to disagree for now."
Words of Unity

## WHAT DO GREAT TEACHERS SAY WHEN...?

A Student Refuses to Cooperate with You and Says, "You're Not My Mom! You Can't Tell Me What To Do! You Can't Make Me Do This Work!" (Scenario 9.3)

### GTL Reminders to Self:

*Remember...* When middle school and high school students refuse to do their work in front of their peers, be careful not to respond with coercion. Stay calm, remain professional, and use persuasion to offer them a different way of thinking about the importance of the assigned work and why they need to do it.

*Words of Guidance*

*Remember...* Coercion might seem to work in the short term; however, for long-term and real change, consider persuasion instead.

*Words of Hope*

*Remember...* When middle school and high school students refuse to cooperate with you and refuse to do their work, maintain accountability for the student by responding with persuasion rather than coercion. Persuasion will make a personal connection that encourages personal responsibility instead of coercion which uses short repetitive reminders that students often ignore.

*Words of Accountability*

*Remember...* When students experience your consistent accountability and respectful guidance after refusing to do the work, it can encourage and motivate them to complete their work.

*Words of Encouragement*

*Remember...* When students complete their work successfully after refusing to do the work, it can encourage and motivate them to do even better work and demonstrate better behavior.

*Words of Encouragement*

*Remember...* When students feel coerced, they may start to tune out or give up.

Words of Relationship

*Remember...* For optimum learning to occur, think win-win so the teacher wins and the student wins. A win-win solution becomes more likely when students know we are on their side, we understand and validate their feelings, and we will work with them to find a solution.

Words of Relationship

*Remember...* If a student refuses to cooperate with you, don't allow it to become teacher versus student. Keep redirecting everyone back to the lesson and learning.

Words of High Expectations

*Remember...* When we use our power and authority to coerce students into doing something, it might provide a short-term quick fix, but it doesn't empower middle school students to manage themselves in high school or high school students to manage themselves for a lifetime.

Words of Respect

*Remember...* Antagonistic words are destructive; they build walls and cause people to act out in ways that can negatively impact learning and relationships. Constructive Words of Grace build relationships and cause people to act in ways that are more positive and uplifting.

Words of Grace

*Remember...* Some of your students will view your authority as you trying to be their parent, and it's important to share how you'll be working with their parents to support their success.

Words of Unity

### GTL to Share with Students:

"You're right; I can't make you do your work. It is your choice whether you do your work. My job is not to make you do your work—my job is to teach you how to do it and then help you along the way. Please let me know if you need my help."

Words of Accountability

"You're right; I can't make you do your work. However, remember this assignment is due on Wednesday. So let me know what your plan is for completing it and if you need my help."

Words of Accountability

(A student says, "You're not my mom! You can't tell me what to do!") "You're right; I am not your mom. But when you are in my class, I am responsible for you, and I care about you. My job is to work with your mom (and your family) to support you and help you learn as much as you can."

Words of Love

"I agree. I can't make you do anything. I can respectfully offer you the choices to choose from—and hopefully you'll make a great choice!"

Words of Respect

(A student who refuses to get started on a project) "This project might feel like too much work for you right now, but you'll be so happy and proud of yourself when it's done—and that you've done your best. Let me know how I can help."

Words of Grace

(A student continuously says, "I am not going to do this work.") "Can you help me understand what it is about this work that keeps you from doing it? Is it too hard? Too easy? Are you not interested in it? Let's take some time now to work out a plan for helping you to do your work in this class."

Words of Understanding

(Talking individually with a student) "I asked you to step outside the room because I didn't want to single you out in class. Your behavior just now was disrespectful to me, and it's not how we agreed to treat each other at the beginning of the year. What's going on? Is everything OK?"

Words of Respect

(Whispering to a student) "Did I do or say something that might have made you say that?"

Words of Understanding

"I noticed you've stopped doing your work today. When I was in middle school or high school, I remember I really struggled with (share a specific struggle you had), and I wanted to give up. I'm so glad that I didn't. I know you can do this—so don't give up!"

Words of Encouragement

(A student says, 'I'm not doing this—I am dropping out of school when I am 16 anyway.') "It's your choice whether or not you drop out of school, but I'm going to try my best to change your mind and make learning interesting, relevant, and engaging for everyone. I hope my class will be a catalyst for finding your interests and passions so you can find a great job when you graduate."

Words of Hope

**GTL to Use When Talking and Communicating with Parents:**

**Proactive phone call to understand why a student is refusing to cooperate with you in the classroom: A student refuses to cooperate with you and says, "You're not my mom! You can't tell me what to do! You can't make me do this work!"**

(Note: This GTL phone conversation provides a template you can modify and send to parents as a letter, email, text message, etc.).

"Hello! My name is…. I'm Jamie's teacher. He's not in trouble. Is now a good time for us to talk?"

Words of Respect

"I enjoy having Jamie in my class. He is… (share something personal, positive, and specific that you've experienced with Jamie and link it to a positive quality that could help Jamie in his future in high school, college and/or career, and life)."

Words of Encouragement

"Since the first day of school, we have been talking about respectful behaviors in the classroom and the importance of showing respect to one another. We've also talked about the importance of keeping a positive teacher–student relationship. I'm calling you to share something that happened today. Jamie was refusing to do his work and was disrespectful to me about it."

Words of Accountability

"I talked with Jamie to get an understanding about his behavior. I asked Jamie to help me understand what it is about the work that keeps him from doing it: Is it too hard? Too easy? Is he not interested in it? I also asked him if there's anything I've said or done that would make him act this way."

Words of Understanding

"He didn't seem to want to talk with me about it, so I wanted to reach out to you to get a better understanding of how he's feeling about school and his work. Is there anything you can share or that you've heard him say that would help me know how to encourage Jamie with his schoolwork?"

Words of Unity

"At the beginning of the school year at the Parent Open House, we talked about the importance of maintaining a strong relationship and open communication between home and school. That's why I called today to share this update about Jamie."

Words of Relationship

"Please let me know if you have any questions at all. My hope is for all our students to feel safe, enjoy school, learn as much as they can every day, and be ready for high school and life (use this with middle school students) or college and/or career and life (use this with high school students)."

Words of Hope

## WHAT DO GREAT TEACHERS SAY WHEN…?

**A Student is Outwardly Angry and Blatantly Disrespectful Toward You. (Scenario 9.4)**

### GTL Reminders to Self:

*Remember…* When addressing a blatantly disrespectful middle school or high school student, it is best to use quieter respectful accountability statements (e.g., "Your behavior right now is not respectful, and we need to talk about what's going on") rather than louder disrespectful accountability statements.

Words of Accountability

*Remember…* If you hold a grudge toward a student who is blatantly disrespectful toward you, it can impact your ability to be objective in dealing with that student.

Words of Grace

*Remember…* Sometimes a student's outward defiance can be a sign that the student is having difficulty with the vocabulary in the text, is not understanding a concept, or is bored with the lesson.

Words of Understanding

*Remember…* Sometimes when students feel powerless in other relationships, they displace their feelings of frustration and defiance with their other relationships and take it out on a teacher.

Words of Understanding

*Remember…* A sudden change in behavior or a pattern of aggression can indicate a student's need for your help and attention.

Words of Relationship

*Remember…* Our goal is to help students learn how to work through their anger and defiance to develop self-management for success in middle school, high school, college and/or career, and life.

Words of Hope

**GTL to Share with Students:**

"Jamie, that behavior is unacceptable, and it's not how we agreed to treat each other when we set up our classroom behavior expectations for how to respect one another."

Words of Accountability

(Student refuses to leave the classroom to discuss misbehavior) "I really believe this is a situation that we can work out without getting the principal involved. It's up to you. If we can't discuss this privately and respectfully in the hallway—then you don't leave me a choice. We'll have to go talk with the principal to find a solution."

Words of Respect

(Student returns from an out-of-school suspension for a disrespectful act toward you.) "We missed you—I am glad you are back."
Words of Grace

"Help me understand what's going on. It seems like you are having a tough day."
Words of Understanding

(Shared with the whole class) "Whenever any of you starts to get angry, I want you to know I am here to help. So if I ask you 'What's going on?', it's because I want to understand what is making you angry, so we can address it and you can keep learning in my class."
Words of High Expectations

(Quieter response to an angry and disrespectful student) "It seems like you might be struggling today? How can I help you work through what's troubling you today?"
Words of Hope

(Individual conversation with angry student) "I can see something has you really upset. We can discuss it together, or you can go to the guidance counselor to talk it out. I don't want to see your anger get you into trouble."
Words of Guidance

(Shared with the whole class) "When anger happens in our class, I don't want to respond to anyone's anger with my own anger. My goal is to stay calm and focus on how to help you work through your anger."
Words of Love

(Individual conversation with student) "If you are feeling angry when you get to school, you need to come

and tell me. We can decide together how to solve your problem."
Words of Relationship

"I know you are angry, and I understand why you would feel that way. However, you and I need to talk about a way to help you control that anger."
Words of Guidance

(Whispering to a student) "Why don't you and I go out in the hallway and try to talk calmly?"
Words of Love

**GTL to Use When Talking and Communicating with Parents:**

**Phone call to discuss a student's behavior in the classroom: A student is angry and blatantly disrespectful toward you.**

(Note: This GTL phone conversation provides a template you can modify and send to parents as a letter, email, text message, etc.).

"Hello! My name is…. I'm Jamie's teacher. Is now a good time for us to talk?"
Words of Respect

"I'm calling to share something that happened today at school. Jamie was angry and disrespectful toward me in class." (State the specific inappropriate behavior.)
Words of Accountability

"I talked with Jamie to get an understanding about his behavior. I asked Jamie to help me understand why he was so angry. I asked him if he was angry with me or with another student or if he was angry about the work. I also asked him if there's anything I've said or done that would make him act this way."
Words of Understanding

"I want to get to the root of Jamie's anger and for him to know that I'm not upset with him; however, his behavior was not acceptable."
Words of Grace

"So I wanted to reach out and make you aware of his behavior and work together to get to the bottom of what is going on with Jamie. Has Jamie shared anything with you about me, or about our class, that could give us a better understanding of how he's feeling about school?"
Words of Understanding

"We have school policies to make sure our school is a safe place for everyone, and the school's policy is clear about a student's blatant disrespect to a teacher." (Share your school's policy for this type of behavior.)
Words of Accountability

"Before we finish our conversation, I wanted to share that I have enjoyed having Jamie in my class. He is… (share something personal, positive, and specific that you've experienced with Jamie and link it to a positive quality that could help Jamie in his future in high school, college and/or career, and life)."
Words of Encouragement

"At the beginning of the school year at the Parent Open House, we talked about the importance of maintaining a strong relationship and open communication between home and school."
Words of Relationship

"Please let me know if you have any questions at all. My hope is for all our students to feel safe, enjoy school, learn as much as they can every day, and be ready for high school and life (use this with middle school students) or college and/or career and life (use this with high school students)."
Words of Hope

## GTL Classroom Activities to Transform Middle School and High School Student Behavior and Your Classroom Culture

### GTL Classroom Activities for Middle School and High School Students who are Uncooperative or Challenge You

We see these activities as either "in the moment" or a time to pull your students together for classroom conversations to encourage student voice and student engagement in your classroom.

We see the teacher as a facilitator and co-learner during these GTL activities and students as active participants in learning how to "see the classroom through the lens of the teacher" and how to manage their own current behavior for success and their future behavior as they get ready for high school, college and/or a career.

1. What does a Win-Win Teacher–Student Relationship Look Like and Sound Like? (Role-Play GTL Scenario for students who are disrespectfully uncooperative with the teacher and determine a Win-Win Teacher–Student outcome) Select one student to role-play a teacher and one student to role-play a student who refuses to cooperate with you and says, "You're not my mom! You can't tell me what to do! You can't make me do this work!" Allow time for the role-playing teacher to respond to the uncooperative student. After the role-play, ask the students who "won" the role-play. Did the teacher win? Why or why not? Did the student win? Why or why not? What does it sound like and look like for the teacher *and* the student to win? Encourage the other students in the class to help the role-playing teacher with what to say and how to respectfully respond to the uncooperative student for a win-win solution. You, as the teacher, will provide a Win-Win Solution if the students do not provide win-win examples. Conclude the role-playing activity with a discussion of how you, as the teacher, have a goal for always having Win-Win outcomes for every situation in the classroom. Also, remind students how even though

you're not their parent, you will work with their family to support them and help them learn as much as they can.

2. (Hit the Pause Button for Discussion on Student Behavior Expectations Related to Respectfully Sharing Disagreements and Opinions with Others When You See Students Having Disrespectful Disagreements in the Classroom with You and Other Students) Share with the students that you are going to "Hit the Pause Button" on the lesson and take important time to discuss how to respectfully share disagreements and opinions with others. Also share with them, if this type of disrespect happens, how you will respectfully hold them accountable for their disrespect, redirect them back to the lesson, and remind them of the class expectation of showing mutual respect. Ask the whole class for their personal answers for *why* it is important to share their disagreements and opinions with others, respectfully—and *how* they share their disagreements and opinions, respectfully. Conclude the discussion by sharing with the students how *you* share *your* disagreements and opinions respectfully and why this respectful approach is important to their future success in high school, college and/or career, and life.

3. (Getting Ready for Life Discussion about Self-Management Strategies for Dealing with Anger and Making Great Choices) Share with the students that you're about to have a Getting Ready for Life discussion related to self-management strategies for dealing with anger and making great choices. Share with your students and spend time discussing how anger can negatively impact their life and future. Then, break the class into small discussion groups. First, ask students to share their thoughts about how anger has negatively impacted their relationships and life with their small group. Circulate around the classroom to listen in on the small group discussions. Allow time for students to share their personal success stories and examples of self-management strategies they've used to prevent and deal with their own anger. Bring the whole class back together and ask if any

group wants to share with the whole class. Remind students how their personal success stories might help and encourage other students to choose self-management strategies when dealing with anger. Conclude the discussion by sharing how making great choices and choosing to manage their own anger will set them up for success for high school, college and/or career, and life.

# 10

# What Do Great Teachers Say When a Student Conflict Occurs?

What do you say when you observe a conflict between two middle school or high school students in your classroom? The student conflict scenarios in this chapter will range from smaller disagreements to students pushing, shoving, and hitting each other, to bullying, to actual physical fighting, and finally to a scenario where a student hits the teacher. If, or when, these student conflict scenarios happen, they can cause significant stress for you and your students. Hopefully, the Great Teacher Language (GTL) examples in this chapter will offer guidance and understanding for you, your students, and parents during these potentially very stressful situations.

This chapter provides teacher-friendly charts with GTL Reminders to Self, GTL to Share with Students, GTL to Use When Talking and Communicating with Parents, and GTL Classroom Activities specifically related to the following:

- Scenario 10.1: Two Students Are in a Small Disagreement and Are Not Getting Along With One Another.
- Scenario 10.2: Two Students Are Arguing with One Another.
- Scenario 10.3: A Student Pushes and/or Shoves Another Student.
- Scenario 10.4: A Student Hits Another Student.

**Scenario 10.5**:  A Student is Bullying Another Student.
**Scenario 10.6**:  A Student is Cyberbullying Another Student.
**Scenario 10.7**:  Two Students Are Physically Fighting.
**Scenario 10.8**:  A Student Hits the Teacher.

> We know these are not the only student conflict behaviors that happen in your classroom. These specific scenarios are a starting point for you to develop your GTL for your classroom. For some of our student behavior scenarios, we have included GTL examples for you to use when talking with parents. These GTL examples are templates for phone conversations, emails, or other types of messages to develop strong communication between teachers and parents and to promote understanding, relationships, trust, and collaboration.

With the many different needs, backgrounds, personalities, quirks, and idiosyncrasies among your middle school and high school students, conflicts are going to happen. Student conflicts range from small disagreements to bullying behaviors to actual physical fighting. Unless we take steps to prevent, defuse, and resolve student conflicts, they are bound to erupt into behaviors that are more frequent and intense. Your Language of Practice (LoP) in the form of GTL can offer these students in conflict the accountability, encouragement, grace, guidance, high expectations, hope, love, relationships, respect, understanding, and unity they need to help them work through their initial differences to prevent greater conflicts from occurring. This GTL can promote patience, love, grace, agreement, cooperation, teamwork, and the power of forgiveness to ensure unity in the classroom.

At any given moment, a conflict can occur in the classroom, and teachers need a plan to prevent conflicts from happening, defuse conflicts in the moment, and promote unity by guiding students through the reconciliation process. This GTL plan begins by actively pursuing an in-depth understanding of student behaviors that lead to conflict. The following list illustrates a host of reasons that lead to student conflict in the classroom:

| | |
|---|---|
| Anger | Feeling wounded |
| Bragging | Fighting for possessions |
| Bullying | Greed |
| Competitiveness | Jealousy |
| Disappointment | Misplaced anger |
| Embarrassment | Misplaced revenge |
| Fear | Rejection |
| Feeling disrespected | Seeking power |
| Feeling insulted | Seeking superiority |
| Feeling offended | Selfishness |
| Feeling sick | Wanting revenge |

When teachers begin to understand the many reasons for middle school and high school student conflict in their classroom, they are better able to help their students learn to avoid conflict with others now and in their future. Showing students a better way to react before a conflict occurs and recognizing students who make positive choices to avoid conflicts are concrete steps in preventing student conflicts. Teachers need to provide opportunities for students to openly discuss the reasons for conflict and then role-play with students on how to avoid conflicts before they happen. (At the end of this chapter, see GTL Classroom Activity entitled "Role-Play GTL Scenario for Students to Practice How to Avoid Conflicts Before They Happen.")

Many of the student conflicts in middle schools and high schools begin with students who are angry and act out their aggression on others. Sometimes students with angry and aggressive behaviors create a wall between themselves and the outside world. When others try to find a way in which to help, they are met with "Don't mess with me." Often students who display these angry and aggressive behaviors do not see the negative consequences of their own behaviors and how those behaviors affect others and their relationships with others.

How do we intentionally break the cycle of student anger and aggression? Teachers need to offer these middle school and high school students concrete and effective strategies for dealing with their anger and aggression. Teachers need to work carefully and persistently with these students, paying special attention to each student's needs. For example, if the student demonstrates a pattern of anger and aggression, then the teacher can refer the student to a guidance counselor or school social worker. These students need to know that they "belong" and that they have a team of support rallying around them. They need to know that others are concerned about them and want to help them. Once these students begin to learn how to deal with their anger, they can begin to break the cycle of anger and aggression. Breaking this cycle of anger and aggression sets them up for success in high school, college and/or career, and life.

Tragically, a significantly large number of student conflicts in middle schools and high schools are related to bullying or cyberbullying behaviors or both. Teachers need to recognize the short-term and lasting impact that bullying and cyberbullying can have on their students. Students who are being bullied may feel threatened and fearful at school, and these threatening and fearful feelings can follow them in their life and their future. Also, a bullied student's ability to focus on their learning, in the present, is disrupted by the words and actions of a bully.

How do we intentionally break the bullying and cyberbullying cycle that leads to students in conflict? What are you going to say to a bully? How will you address the needs of the student being bullied—and the bully? Both the person being bullied and the bully need your words of grace, hope, love, and accountability.

The bully must be held accountable. Middle school and high school students need to know that bullying is not acceptable—*ever*. It's not acceptable in the classroom or outside the classroom. It's not acceptable on any digital device. They need to see the impact of "acting out" or "typing out" their aggression and the hurt it causes others and accept the consequences for their behavior. They also need clear alternatives for working through their aggressive feelings and strategies for restoring relationships. A teacher's quick, kind, consistent, and firm response to bullying and cyberbullying behaviors can offer a way to end the cycle of bullying in the classroom and hopefully makes the classroom a safer place for everyone.

The middle school and high school student being bullied needs your support and guidance as well. Your words and actions can offer them the confidence and encouragement to overcome their feelings of fear and revenge. When the student being bullied sees your quick, kind, consistent, and firm response to eliminating bullying behavior, that student—and everyone in the classroom—sees that bullying is unacceptable and the classroom becomes a safer place for learning.

Even with the best prevention plans, there will be conflicts that escalate into major classroom disruptions with intense emotions and physical fighting. When these major disruptions occur, teachers need to immediately intervene with a plan to defuse the situation. Defusing a student conflict is more effective when the teacher has provided and discussed clear expectations for behavior and the consequences for fighting and bullying. (At the end of this chapter, see GTL Classroom Activity entitled Hit the Pause Button for Discussion on Student Behavior Expectations Related to Your School's Policies on Bullying, Cyberbullying, and Fighting and What to Do if You are Bullied and How to Prevent a Fight.) The teacher's response needs to be calm, caring, impartial, and poised. Our language and actions need to convey to students that "I'm concerned for each of you. I really want to know what's going on here, but we all need to take a step back and cool down. Then, we'll come together to discuss the problem."

When middle school and high school students are experiencing intense emotions from a physical conflict, they need time to cool down and regain their composure. Their brains need time to make the mental and emotional shift to re-engage in a helpful conversation about what really happened. By separating students and giving them time to cool down, we increase the likelihood of a rational and honest discussion at a later time. Once the cool-down period is over, students need to know the teacher's ultimate goal is to understand the reason for the physical conflict and help students work through it. Therefore, teachers need to listen to both sides of the situation and respect the feelings and opinions of everyone involved.

Whether they know it or not, middle school and high school students in conflict have four specific needs:

1. The need to be heard. All students need to know they will be given the opportunity to share their side of the story without interruption and with a sincere attempt to listen for understanding.
2. The need to hear the other person's side of the story. When we challenge students to listen to each other and put themselves in the other person's situation, they learn a valuable life lesson regarding empathy and understanding.
3. The need for the truth to rise to the top. Getting to the truth can be difficult. The feelings and emotions surrounding conflict can cloud judgment and create confusion. Sometimes students have forgotten the original reason for their disagreement. Often other students are stirring the conflict. To get to the truth, teachers need to insist on honesty and encourage students to reflect on the past events that led to their conflict—what really happened.
4. The need for reconciliation. Students in conflict need to experience reconciliation with one another. What better life lesson can a student learn in your classroom than the one that teaches them they can move from frustration to friendship, anger to understanding, and conflict to unity?

Conflict will not resolve itself, however, and middle school and high school students need a teacher's guidance to move toward reconciliation. When students experience the opportunity to resolve their conflict with unity as the goal, it takes the focus off themselves, and they begin to see their responsibility to other people in their current classroom community, the larger school community, and their future life. They are more likely to value and appreciate others and experience the benefits of working, learning, and living in a unified classroom, community, and world.

## WHAT DO GREAT TEACHERS SAY WHEN...?

**Two Students Are in a Small Disagreement and Are Not Getting Along With One Another. (Scenario 10.1)**

### GTL Reminders to Self:

*Remember...* Provide clear examples and strategies for middle school and high school students to follow when they feel a problem or disagreement is starting.
Words of Guidance

*Remember...* Let your students know you care about them and you will treat them all the same way.
Words of Love

*Remember...* There's a reason why middle school and high school students may have small disagreements, so try to find out what's going on and what is driving those behaviors.
Words of Understanding

*Remember...* If a student doesn't want to share what's wrong, don't force the issue. Be ready to listen when they are ready to talk.
Words of Relationship

*Remember...* By proactively surveying the classroom and school landscape to determine the relationship needs of your students and nurturing the growth of friendly relationships among your students, you can possibly help prevent small student disagreements.
Words of Understanding

*Remember...* A small disagreement can occur quickly in the classroom, and teachers need a plan to prevent them from happening, defuse the disagreement in the moment, and promote unity by guiding students through the reconciliation process.
Words of Unity

**GTL to Share with Students:**

"To maintain unity in our class, it's important for us to talk through our arguments with respect and understanding."

Words of Grace

"If you have a problem or disagreement with someone, you need to respectfully talk with that person to understand their side of the story. Listening and understanding how they feel can help you get along with each other."

Words of Guidance

"When you have a small disagreement with another student, be careful not to listen to the disrespectful or untrue things that other students might be saying about it. Instead, listen to students whom you trust and who are encouraging you to talk to the other student to work it out."

Words of High Expectations

(Speaking privately with a student) "When you say those things to (that other student), it shows disrespect for him/her. What could you have said instead?"

Words of Respect

(Shared with the whole class) "I want all of us to work through our differences so we can work together and learn together."

Words of Unity

(Shared with the whole class) "The class rules and behavior expectations we agreed on at the beginning of the year help us get along better with each other."

Words of Guidance

(Shared with the whole class) "When you have a problem with another student in our class, I'm going to ask you both to figure out a solution together."
Words of Accountability

(To the two students in a disagreement) "I noticed the two of you have not come to an agreement, yet. I want to talk with you both about the situation so we can figure out a solution together."
Words of Relationship

(Shared with the whole class) "I care about all of you, and I want you all to be successful in life, so I'm going to hold each of you accountable for the choices you make."
Words of Love

(A student overcomes peer pressure and chooses to help another student.) "I heard how you handled that situation with the other student. It took a lot of courage to do the right thing, and I am really proud of you!"
Words of Encouragement

## WHAT DO GREAT TEACHERS SAY WHEN...?

**Two Students Are Arguing with One Another. (Scenario 10.2)**

### GTL Reminders to Self:

*Remember...* There is a reason why middle school and high school students act the way they do, so try to find out what's going on and what is driving those behaviors.
Words of Understanding

*Remember...* Arguments sometimes happen because there is a misunderstanding between two students.
Words of Guidance

*Remember...* Be careful not to make assumptions about students and their circumstances. Instead, develop meaningful relationships with them that encourage current and future success.

Words of Relationship

*Remember...* When students are emotionally charged, you can sometimes defuse the situation by asking the students to help you with something and then thanking them for their help.

Words of Guidance

*Remember...* Survey the class and school landscape and look for signs of student disagreements and be ready to offer students strategies to avoid verbal arguments.

Words of Hope

*Remember...* An argument between two students can occur quickly in the classroom, and teachers need a plan to prevent arguments from happening, defuse them in the moment, and promote unity by guiding students through the reconciliation process.

Words of Unity

### GTL to Share with Students:

"There might be times when you get so angry with another student that you want to yell at them. But rather than doing that, take a step back, breathe, and take a minute to consider forgiving them."

Words of Grace

"When others are arguing with you and accusing you of something you haven't done, don't lash out and get defensive; instead, respectfully explain yourself and explain why you would not do that."

Words of Guidance

"I thought you were going to react differently in your group work today. I was glad to see you made the choice to complete your work instead of getting into an argument with those other students. I'm proud of you."

Words of Encouragement

"Yesterday I saw you talking to (the other student) about the issue between the two of you. We've been discussing ways to work through conflicts together in our class. When I saw you making the effort to get along, I was proud of you."

Words of Encouragement

"You both obviously have strong feelings about this issue. I'm hoping the two of you can work it out together now, but if that's not possible, then the three of us will need to discuss these feelings and work together to resolve this problem."

Words of Guidance

"I can't allow this loud arguing in our classroom. You can cool down here and re-engage in the lesson, or talk with me calmly in the hallway, or we can go and talk with the assistant principal or the guidance counselor. Which would you rather do? It's your choice."

Words of Accountability

"I have seen you handle this type of situation before. I know you can do it again. Let's talk about how you can make this right with (the other student)."

Words of Hope

"Help me understand why you're so angry with (another student). We need to get to the bottom of this issue—so we can focus on our lesson. I'm wondering if it's a complete misunderstanding."

Words of Understanding

(Shared with the whole class when you observe all students positively working in groups) "I'm excited to see everyone working so hard on these group projects!"
Words of Encouragement

**GTL to Use When Talking and Communicating with Parents:**

**Phone call to discuss a student's behavior in the classroom: A student is arguing with other students and disrupting class multiple times during the day.**

(Note: This GTL phone conversation provides a template you can modify and send to parents as a letter, email, text message, etc.).

"Hello! My name is…. I'm Jamie's teacher. Is now a good time for us to talk?"
Words of Respect

"I enjoy having Jamie in my class. He is… (share something personal, positive, and specific that you've experienced with Jamie and link it to a positive quality that could help Jamie in his future in high school, college and/or career, and life)."
Words of Encouragement

"At the beginning of the school year at the Parent Open House, you and I talked about the importance of maintaining a strong relationship and open communication between home and school. That's why I called today to share something that happened several times in class today. Jamie was arguing with different students and disrupting class and the learning."
Words of Accountability

"I talked with Jamie to get an understanding about his behavior. I asked Jamie to help me understand why he was arguing so much today. I asked him if he was frustrated or angry or didn't feel well. I also asked him if there's anything another student has done to cause him to argue this way."

Words of Understanding

"I want to get to the root of Jamie's arguing and for him to know that I'm not upset with him; however, his behavior was not acceptable, and it's negatively impacting his schoolwork."

Words of Understanding

"So I wanted to reach out and make you aware of his behavior and work together to get to the bottom of what is going on with Jamie. Has Jamie shared anything with you about our class, or other students in our class, that could give us a better understanding of how he's feeling about school?"

Words of Understanding

"Please let me know if you have any questions at all. My hope is for all our students to feel safe, enjoy school, learn as much as they can every day, and be ready for high school and life (use this with middle school students) or college and/or career and life (use this with high school students)."

Words of Hope

## WHAT DO GREAT TEACHERS SAY WHEN...?

**A Student Pushes and/or Shoves Another Student. (Scenario 10.3)**

### GTL Reminders to Self:

*Remember...* If the circumstances around middle school and high school students pushing and shoving are unclear, get as close to the truth of the matter as possible, discuss the inappropriateness of the behavior, then offer both students the opportunity to talk it through together, and defuse the situation rather than have it escalate.

Words of Unity

*Remember...* Some students may need to talk with you to discuss a problem they are having with another student.

Words of Relationship

*Remember...* Offer students a listening ear whenever they come to you to discuss a problem they are having with another student.

Words of Relationship

*Remember...* Be aware of the situations throughout the school day that lend themselves to pushing and shoving (e.g., getting up out of their seats and leaving class, walking down the hallways, coming into class, in the cafeteria, in the gym and locker room).

Words of Guidance

*Remember...* Sometimes students act out anger and push other students because of physical problems or they don't feel good. They might need to talk to you or see the school nurse.

Words of Understanding

**GTL to Share with Students:**

"If you need somebody to talk to or you've got a problem that you think might cause you to act out in class, then come pull me to the side one-on-one before we get class started."

Words of Guidance

"I care about both of you, so I'm going to hold you both accountable for pushing and shoving each other. We need to talk together about what happened, how

the pushing and shoving started, and we'll also talk about how to make sure this doesn't happen again."
Words of Love

"I really want to understand what's going on and what caused you to push that other student. I want to help you make it right with the other student and keep it from happening again."
Words of Relationship

"You are obviously too angry to talk about it right now, but once you cool down, we can get to the bottom of the pushing and shoving and eliminate it."
Words of Hope

"Let's start at the beginning—what made you so angry that you would push another student?"
Words of Understanding

"In our classroom, we are going to treat others the way we want to be treated."
Words of High Expectations

## WHAT DO GREAT TEACHERS SAY WHEN...?

**A Student Hits Another Student. (Scenario 10.4)**

### GTL Reminders to Self:

*Remember...* Harsh words of accountability for students who hit another student can lead to students who are angry or withdrawn, and as a result, they focus more on the teacher's disrespect for them rather than on their own misbehavior.
Words of Guidance

*Remember…* Respectfully helping students realize and accept the consequences for their misbehavior can nurture the growth of personal accountability and self-management, right now and for their lifetime.

Words of Accountability

*Remember…* Having a culture of clear and high expectations for student behavior can help prevent misbehaviors before they happen. It allows students "in the moment" to consider the choice to meet those expectations.

Words of High Expectations

*Remember…* It's important for you to make all students aware of the consequences for misbehaviors in your classroom before the misbehaviors happen, especially the consequences if they physically hit another student.

Words of High Expectations

*Remember…* Rather than harboring ill feelings for a student who has hit another student in your classroom, demonstrate grace and dig deep to get at the root of the problem to better understand middle school and high school students' behaviors.

Words of Grace

*Remember…* When dealing with a student who has hit another student, step back, breathe, and speak calmly with the student.

Words of Respect

*Remember…* When middle school and high school students reach a point in time when they are capable of "taking a step back" and recognizing that their behavior is destructive for themselves and others, they are demonstrating characteristics of self-management.

Words of Hope

**GTL to Share with Students:**

(Shared with the whole class) "When you are feeling angry, stop, count to 10, and think about the consequences before you react."
Words of Guidance

(Privately to student who hits another student) "Can you help me understand what's wrong? This isn't like you. Do you want to talk about it?"
Words of Relationship

(Privately to student) "Because you hit another student, we have to discuss your behavior and your consequences with the principal and your parents. We have school policies to make sure our school is a safe place for everyone, and the school's policy is clear about the consequences for hitting another student."
Words of Accountability

"Let's talk together so you can tell me what happened between you and (the other student)."
Words of Understanding

(Privately to both students) "I care about both of you, and I want to help you both work this out. So how can the three of us work this out so it won't happen anymore?"
Words of Unity

"I'm glad we worked together on this plan for improving your behavior. I know it's going to work because you are a very determined person and when you give your attention to something, you get it done!"
Words of Encouragement

**GTL to Use When Talking and Communicating with Parents:**

**Phone call to discuss a student's behavior in the classroom: A student hits another student in your class.**

(This phone call is coming from the principal's office. The principal and the teacher agree the teacher will lead the phone conversation.)

"Hello! My name is…. I'm Jamie's teacher. Is now a good time for us to talk?"
Words of Respect

"At the beginning of the school year at the Parent Open House, you and I talked about the importance of maintaining a strong relationship and open communication between home and school. That's why I'm calling to share something that happened in class today. Jamie hit another student in class. The first thing I did was to speak to both students to get an understanding of what happened."
Words of Accountability

"Then, I talked with Jamie individually to get an understanding of his behavior. I asked Jamie to help me understand why he hit the other student. I asked him if he was frustrated or angry or didn't feel well. I also asked Jamie if there was anything the other student did to cause him to hit the other student."
Words of Understanding

"I have Jamie here in the principal's office with me. He's going to tell you what happened."
Words of Accountability

(Jamie tells his parents what happened and is truthful.)

"We have school policies to make sure our school is a safe place for everyone, and the school's policy is clear about the consequences for hitting another student." (State your school's policy for this type of behavior.)
Words of Accountability

"I want to get to the root of Jamie's behavior and for him to know that I'm not upset with him; however, his behavior was not acceptable, and it's negatively impacting his schoolwork."
Words of Understanding

"So I wanted to reach out and make you aware of his behavior and work together to get to the bottom of what is going on with Jamie. Has Jamie shared anything with you about our class, or other students in our class, that could give us a better understanding of how he's feeling about school?"
Words of Understanding

"Before we finish our conversation, I wanted to share that I have enjoyed having Jamie in my class. He is… (share something personal, positive, and specific that you've experienced with Jamie and link it to a positive quality that could help Jamie in his future in high school, college and/or career, and life)."
Words of Encouragement

"Please let me know if you have any questions at all. My hope is for all our students to feel safe, enjoy school, learn as much as they can every day, and be ready for high school and life (use this with middle school students) or college and/or career and life (use this with high school students)."
Words of Hope

**GTL to Use When Talking and Communicating with Parents:**

**Phone call to the parent of a student who was hit by another student in class.**

**(The student who has been hit wants to call their parents to let them know they are OK and to share what happened.)**

"Hello! My name is…. I'm Mark's teacher. He's not in trouble. Is now a good time for us to talk?"
Words of Respect

"I'm calling you to share something that happened in class today. Another student in our class hit Mark. He's here with me and he wants to talk with you about what happened."
Words of Understanding

(Mark tells his parents what happened and is truthful.)

"The first thing I did was to speak to both students to get an understanding of what happened."
Words of Accountability

"Then, I talked with Mark individually to get an understanding of how he's feeling about it. I asked him if he was hurt, needed to go to the nurse, or call home. He wanted to talk with you about it."
Words of Understanding

"We have school policies to make sure our school is a safe place for everyone, and the school's policy is clear about the consequences for hitting another student."
Words of Accountability

"Before we finish our conversation, I wanted to share that I have enjoyed having Mark in my class. He is… (share something personal, positive, and specific that you've experienced with Mark and link it to a positive quality that could help Mark in his future in high school, college and/or career, and life)."
Words of Encouragement

"Please let me know if you have any questions at all. My hope is for all our students to feel safe, enjoy

school, learn as much as they can every day, and be ready for high school and life (use this with middle school students) or college and/or career and life (use this with high school students)."

Words of Hope

## WHAT DO GREAT TEACHERS SAY WHEN...?

**A Student is Bullying Another Student. (Scenario 10.5)**

### GTL Reminders to Self:

*Remember...* Rather than harboring ill feelings for the students who are bullying other students, separate the student from the bullying behaviors, demonstrate grace to them, and dig deep to get to the root of the problem.

Words of Grace

*Remember...* When you are working with a student who is demonstrating bullying behaviors, address the bullying behaviors but don't label the student as a bully.

Words of Love

*Remember...* Sometimes you—alone—cannot solve a student's problem; you will need the help of the guidance counselor and other support personnel.

Words of Guidance

*Remember...* Wanting to get to the root of the problem when dealing with student bullying is a sign of care and love.

Words of Love

*Remember...* No one likes to feel threatened. The student being bullied needs your quick, kind, consistent, and ongoing attention and support.

Words of Relationship

*Remember…* Students who bully others may have been bullied themselves.

Words of Understanding

*Remember…* Be on the lookout and listen for potential bullying behavior. Sometimes students who are being bullied start to withdraw and get silent. Your whole class can feel unsafe and be negatively impacted by bullying behavior.

Words of Guidance

**GTL to Share with Students:**

(Shared with the whole class) "I want this to be very clear to everyone. Our class is going to be a safe place, and bullying will not be tolerated."

Words of Accountability

(Shared with the whole class) "If another student is bullying you, here's what you need to do to stay safe and confident in our classroom. First, ask them respectfully to stop. If they refuse to stop, then you come to me, and we'll work through the problem and eliminate it."

Words of Guidance

"If you're being bullied, be sure not to keep your angry or scared feelings inside without sharing them with me or another adult. It's important to let someone know how you are feeling, so they can help you with the problem."

Words of Guidance

"Be careful when you start to compare yourself to others. It could lead to feelings of insecurity and jealousy which could lead to bullying behavior and conflicts."

Words of Guidance

(Private conversation with two students about bullying behaviors) "Here's how we're going to discuss what's been happening at school. Each of you will share your side of the story—and I expect both of you to be honest. I also expect each of you to listen respectfully to what the other person is saying and try to put yourself in the other person's place."

Words of Understanding

(Shared with the whole class) "We are going to work together to keep bullying from happening in our classroom. Let's treat others the way you want to be treated, so we can make our class safe and fun for everyone."

Words of High Expectations

(Shared with the whole class) "It is so important for all of us to understand how our words and actions can make others feel sad or angry. Let's remember to stop and think carefully about what we say and what we do to others in our class."

Words of Understanding

(Private conversation with a student) "You seem upset—what's going on? Is someone bothering you?"

Words of Love

(Private conversation with a student who might be bullying another student) "One of your classmates told me they feel like you are bullying them. Let's talk about it. I want to listen to you and try to understand what's going on."

Words of Understanding

**GTL to Use When Talking and Communicating with Parents:**

**Phone call to discuss a student's behavior in the classroom: A student is bullying another student in your class.**

(This phone call is coming from the principal's office. The principal and the teacher agree the teacher will lead the phone conversation.)

"Hello! My name is…. I'm Jamie's teacher. Is now a good time for us to talk?"
Words of Respect

"I have Jamie here in the principal's office with me. He's going to tell you what happened today."
Words of Accountability

(Jamie tells his parents what happened and is truthful.)

"I want to get to the root of Jamie's behavior and for him to know that I'm not upset with him; however, his behavior was not acceptable, and it's negatively impacting his schoolwork."
Words of Understanding

"The first thing I did was to speak to both students to get an understanding of what happened."
Words of Accountability

"Then, I talked with Jamie individually to get an understanding of his behavior. I asked Jamie to help me understand why he was bullying the other student. I asked him if he was frustrated or angry or didn't feel well. I also asked Jamie if there was anything the other student did to cause him to treat the other student that way."
Words of Understanding

"We have school policies to make sure our school is a safe place for everyone, and the school's policy is clear about the consequences for bullying another student." (State your school's policy for this type of behavior.)
Words of Accountability

"I wanted to reach out and make you aware of his behavior and work together to get to the bottom of what is going on with Jamie. Has Jamie shared anything with you about our class, or other students in our class, that could give us a better understanding of how he's feeling about school?"

Words of Understanding

"Before we finish our conversation, I wanted to share that I have enjoyed having Jamie in my class. He is… (share something personal, positive, and specific that you've experienced with Jamie and link it to a positive quality that could help Jamie in his future in high school, college and/or career, and life)."

Words of Encouragement

"Please let me know if you have any questions at all. My hope is for all our students to feel safe, enjoy school, learn as much as they can every day, and be ready for high school and life (use this with middle school students) or college and/or career and life (use this with high school students)."

Words of Hope

**GTL to Use When Talking and Communicating with Parents:**

**Phone call to the parent of a student who has been bullied by another student in class.**

(The student who has been bullied wants to call their parents to let them know they are OK and to share what happened.)

"Hello! My name is…. I'm Mark's teacher. He's not in trouble. Is now a good time for us to talk?"

Words of Respect

"I'm calling you to share something that happened in class today. Another student admitted to bullying Mark in class. The first thing I did was to speak to both students to get an understanding of what happened. Mark's here with me and he wants to talk with you about it."

Words of Understanding

(Mark tells his parents what happened and is truthful.)

"After I talked with both students about what happened, I spoke with Mark individually to get an understanding of what happened to him. I also reassured Mark that bullying behaviors are unacceptable, and we want to make sure he feels cared for and safe at school."

Words of Understanding

"We have school policies to make sure our school is a safe place for everyone, and the school's policy is clear about the consequences for bullying another student."

Words of Accountability

"Before we finish our conversation, I wanted to share that I have enjoyed having Mark in my class. He is… (share something personal, positive, and specific that you've experienced with Mark and link it to a positive quality that could help Mark in his future in high school, college and/or career, and life)."

Words of Encouragement

"Please let me know if you have any questions at all. My hope is for all our students to feel safe, enjoy school, learn as much as they can every day, and be ready for high school and life (use this with middle school students) or college and/or career and life (use this with high school students)."

Words of Hope

## WHAT DO GREAT TEACHERS SAY WHEN...?

**A Student is Cyberbullying Another Student. (Scenario 10.6)**

### GTL Reminders to Self:

*Remember...* Students need to be reminded that it's never OK for students to record videos, take pictures, and post them on social media for the purposes of embarrassing or bullying someone else.

Words of Accountability

*Remember...* Rather than harboring ill feelings for the students who are cyberbullying other students, separate the student from the cyberbullying behaviors, demonstrate grace to them, and dig deep to get to the root of the problem.

Words of Grace

*Remember...* When you are working with a student who is demonstrating cyberbullying behaviors, address the bullying behaviors but don't label the student as a cyberbully.

Words of Love

*Remember...* Sometimes you—alone—cannot solve a student's problem; you will need the help of the guidance counselor and other support personnel.

Words of Guidance

*Remember...* Wanting to get to the root of the problem when dealing with student cyberbullying is a sign of care and love.

Words of Love

*Remember...* No one likes to feel threatened. The student being cyberbullied needs your needs your quick, kind, consistent, and ongoing attention and support.

Words of Relationship

*Remember…* Students who cyberbully others may have been cyberbullied themselves.
Words of Understanding

*Remember…* Be on the lookout and listen for potential cyberbullying behavior. Sometimes students who are being cyberbullied start to withdraw and get silent. Your whole class can feel unsafe and be negatively impacted by cyberbullying behavior.
Words of Guidance

**GTL to Share with Students:**

(Shared with the whole class) "I want this to be very clear to everyone. Our class is going to be a safe place, and cyberbullying will not be tolerated."
Words of Accountability

(Shared with the whole class) "It's never OK for students to record videos, take pictures, and post them on social media for the purposes of embarrassing or bullying someone else."
Words of Accountability

(Shared with the whole class) "If another student is cyberbullying you, here's what you need to do to stay safe and confident at school: come to me immediately and we'll work through the problem and eliminate it."
Words of Guidance

"If you're being cyberbullied, be sure not to keep your angry or scared feelings inside without sharing them with me or another adult. It's important to let someone know how you are feeling, so they can help you with the problem."
Words of Guidance

"Be careful when you start to compare yourself to others. It could lead to feelings of insecurity and jealousy which could lead to cyberbullying behavior and conflicts."
Words of Guidance

(Private conversation with two students about cyberbullying behaviors) "Here's how we're going to discuss what's been happening on your devices. Each of you will share your side of the story—and I expect both of you to be honest. I also expect each of you to listen respectfully to what the other person is saying and try to put yourself in the other person's place."
Words of Understanding

(Shared with the whole class) "We are going to work together to keep cyberbullying from happening in our class. Let's treat others the way you want to be treated, so we can make our class safe and fun for everyone."
Words of High Expectations

(Shared with the whole class) "It is so important for all of us to understand how our words and actions online and in person can make others feel embarrassed, sad, or angry. Let's remember to stop and think carefully about what we say and what we do online and in person to others in our class."
Words of Understanding

(Private conversation with a student who might be cyberbullied) "You seem upset—what's going on? Is someone bothering you?"
Words of Love

(Private conversation with a student who might be cyberbullying another student) "One of your classmates told me they feel like you are cyberbullying them. Let's talk about it. I want to listen to you and try to understand what's going on."
Words of Understanding

**GTL to Use When Talking and Communicating with Parents:**

**Phone call to discuss a student's behavior in the classroom: A student is cyberbullying another student in your class.**

(This phone call is coming from the principal's office. The principal and the teacher agree that the teacher will lead the phone conversation.)

"Hello! My name is…. I'm Jamie's teacher. Is now a good time for us to talk?"
Words of Respect

"I have Jamie here in the principal's office with me. He's going to tell you what happened today."
Words of Accountability

(Jamie tells his parents what happened and is truthful.)

"I want to get to the root of Jamie's behavior and for him to know that I'm not upset with him; however, his behavior was not acceptable, and it's negatively impacting his schoolwork."
Words of Understanding

"The first thing I did was to speak to both students to get an understanding of what happened."
Words of Accountability

"Then, I talked with Jamie individually to get an understanding of his behavior. I asked Jamie to help me understand why he was cyberbullying the other student. I asked him if he was frustrated or angry or didn't feel well. I also asked Jamie if there was anything the other student did to cause him to treat the other student that way."
Words of Understanding

"We have school policies to make sure our school is a safe place for everyone, and the school's policy is clear about the consequences for cyberbullying another student." (State your school's policy for this type of behavior.)

Words of Accountability

"I wanted to reach out and make you aware of his behavior and work together to get to the bottom of what is going on with Jamie. Has Jamie shared anything with you about our class, or other students in our class, that could give us a better understanding of how he's feeling about school?"

Words of Understanding

"Before we finish our conversation, I wanted to share that I have enjoyed having Jamie in my class. He is… (share something personal, positive, and specific that you've experienced with Jamie and link it to a positive quality that could help Jamie in his future in high school, college and/or career, and life)."

Words of Encouragement

"Please let me know if you have any questions at all. My hope is for all our students to feel safe, enjoy school, learn as much as they can every day, and be ready for high school and life (use this with middle school students) or college and/or career and life (use this with high school students)."

Words of Hope

**GTL to Use When Talking and Communicating with Parents:**

**Phone call to the parent of a student who has been cyberbullied by another student in class.**

(The student who has been cyberbullied wants to call their parents to let them know they are OK and to share what happened.)

"Hello! My name is…. I'm Mark's teacher. He's not in trouble. Is now a good time for us to talk?"

Words of Respect

"I'm calling you to share something that happened in class today. Another student admitted to cyberbullying Mark in class. The first thing I did was to speak to both students to get an understanding of what happened. Mark's here with me and he wants to talk with you about it."

Words of Understanding

(Mark tells his parents what happened and is truthful.)

"After I talked with both students about what happened, I spoke with Mark individually to get an understanding of what happened to him. I also reassured Mark that cyberbullying behaviors are unacceptable, and we want to make sure he feels cared for and safe at school."

Words of Understanding

"We have school policies to make sure our school is a safe place for everyone, and the school's policy is clear about the consequences for cyberbullying another student."

Words of Accountability

"Before we finish our conversation, I wanted to share that I have enjoyed having Mark in my class. He is… (share something personal, positive, and specific that you've experienced with Mark and link it to a positive quality that could help Mark in his future in high school, college and/or career, and life)."

Words of Encouragement

"Please let me know if you have any questions at all. My hope is for all our students to feel safe, enjoy

school, learn as much as they can every day, and be ready for high school and life (use this with middle school students) or college and/or career and life (use this with high school students)."

Words of Hope

## WHAT DO GREAT TEACHERS SAY WHEN…?

**Two Students Are Physically Fighting. (Scenario 10.7)**

(This scenario is a serious one. Anytime students fight in your class, it is a chaotic, scary, and emotionally and physically charged experience for the two students, you, and all the students in the class. Engage your school principal and resource officers immediately when student fighting happens in your class, to help you handle the situation. Hopefully, these GTL examples offer guidance and understanding for you during this very stressful experience.)

### GTL Reminders to Self:

*Remember…* Keeping a close watch on possible personal conflicts that might happen between middle school or high school students and redirecting those students in a more positive direction may help prevent the outburst of a physical fight between them.

Words of Guidance

*Remember…* It's important for you to make all students aware of the consequences for fighting in your school. Knowing and understanding the consequences may deter students from making the choice to physically fight with another student.

Words of Accountability

*Remember…* Provide students a list of effective strategies they can use to prevent fighting before it happens (e.g., go to the teacher immediately when you have a conflict with another student, remove yourself from the situation, maintain respect for other students, and talk with the guidance counselor).

*Words of Guidance*

*Remember…* When a physical fight breaks out in your class, remain calm and get help from the principal and assistant principal, immediately.

*Words of Guidance*

*Remember…* When a physical fight breaks out in your class, reassure the other students that you're going to take care of the situation. Remind them they need to stay calm and move away from the fight.

*Words of Guidance*

*Remember…* When students are experiencing intense emotions from a physical conflict, they need time to cool down to regain their composure, and they need a minute to make a mental and emotional shift back to the lesson.

*Words of Grace*

*Remember…* Whether they know it or not, middle school and high school students in conflict have four specific needs: (1) the need to be heard, (2) the need to hear the other person's side of the story, (3) the need for the truth to rise to the top, and (4) the need for reconciliation.

*Words of Love*

*Remember…* Sometimes students act out their anger on others because others have acted out their anger on them.

*Words of Understanding*

### GTL to Share with Students:

"That's unacceptable classroom behavior, so you both need to separate, calm down, regain your composure, and take a minute to make a mental and emotional shift before we talk about what happened."

Words of Accountability

"Obviously there is a problem here. I want to hear both sides of this problem, but first we need to step away and cool off."

Words of Accountability

"Once you've cooled down, we'll have an honest discussion of what happened."

Words of Guidance

I'm concerned for each of you. I really want to know what's going on here, but we all need to take a step back and cool off. Then, we'll come together to discuss the problem."

Words of Unity

"What were you doing when the disagreement started, (Student 1)? What were you doing, (Student 2)? What could you have done differently to keep this from happening?"

Words of Accountability

"Let's talk about what just happened. We need to get the truth of what really happened and then decide what we could have said or done to prevent this fight."

Words of Accountability

"Because you were both fighting, we have to discuss your behavior and your consequences with the principal and your parents. We have school policies to make sure our school is a safe place for everyone, and

the school's policy is clear about the consequences for fighting."
Words of Accountability

"Now that we have cooled down, what can we do to keep this from happening again?"
Words of Understanding

"Because of your behavior, you're going to be (state your school's policy for fighting)". (If your school's policy is an out-of-school suspension, you can say…) "We're going to send home your schoolwork, and you'll keep up with your assignments. We're going to call your parents right now and let you explain to them what happened and what you did."
Words of Accountability

(After the phone call with parents) "I appreciate your being honest with your parents about what happened—that's the first step in getting to the truth of what caused you to act that way. Once we know what caused it, we can learn how to prevent it from happening again."
Words of Encouragement

(Student returns to school after an out-of-school suspension for physical fighting) "I'm glad that you are back—we missed you. I'm looking forward to moving ahead and helping you in any way I can."
Words of Hope

## GTL to Use When Talking and Communicating with Parents:

**Phone call to discuss a student's behavior in the classroom: Two students have been physically fighting in your class.**

(This phone call is coming from the principal's office. The principal and the teacher agree that the teacher will lead the phone conversation. The phone call is made to each student's parents individually).

"Hello! My name is…. I'm Jamie's teacher. Is now a good time for us to talk?"

Words of Respect

"I'm calling to share something that happened in class today. Jamie got into a physical fight with another student in our class. I have Jamie here in the principal's office with me. He's going to tell you what happened."

(Jamie tells his parents what happened and is truthful.)

"I want you to know, the first thing I did was to speak to both students to get an understanding of what happened."

Words of Accountability

"Then, I talked with Jamie individually to get an understanding of his behavior. I asked Jamie to help me understand what caused him to get into a fight with the other student. I asked him if he was frustrated or angry or didn't feel well. I also asked Jamie if there was anything the other student did to cause him to fight the other student."

Words of Understanding

"We have school policies to make sure our school is a safe place for everyone, and the school's policy is clear about the consequences for fighting with another student. Because of Jamie's behavior, he's going to be (state your school's policy for fighting)". (If your school's policy is an out-of-school suspension, you can say…) "An out-of-school suspension doesn't mean he'll get behind in his schoolwork. We're going to send home his schoolwork, and he'll be able to keep up with his assignments."

Words of Accountability

"I want to get to the root of Jamie's behavior and for him to know that I'm not upset with him; however, his behavior was not acceptable, and it's negatively impacting his schoolwork.".

Words of Understanding

"I wanted to reach out and make you aware of his behavior and work together to get to the bottom of what is going on with Jamie. Has Jamie shared anything with you about our class, or other students in our class, that could give us a better understanding of how he's feeling about school? If he shares more with you while he's home, please let me know. I really want to understand what caused this and how to keep it from happening again."

Words of Understanding

"Before we finish our conversation, I wanted to share that I have enjoyed having Jamie in my class. He is… (share something personal, positive, and specific that you've experienced with Jamie and link it to a positive quality that could help Jamie in his future in high school, college and/or career, and life)."

Words of Encouragement

"Please let me know if you have any questions at all. My hope is for all our students to feel safe, enjoy school, learn as much as they can every day, and be ready for high school and life (use this with middle school students) or college and/or career and life (use this with high school students)."

Words of Hope

## WHAT DO GREAT TEACHERS SAY WHEN…?

**A Student Hits the Teacher. (Scenario 10.8)**

(A student hits you! We're so sorry. This scenario is a personal one—and a serious one.

Anytime you get hit by a student—whether it's a slap on your arm unexpectedly or a more intense and aggressive act—it's physically and emotionally hurtful. Hopefully, these GTL examples offer encouragement and hope for you during this very stressful experience.)

**GTL Reminders to Self:**

*Remember…* In this type of situation, no one expects you to handle it perfectly. Protect yourself, protect the other students, and show yourself grace as you do the best you can.

Words of Love

*Remember…* Do not retaliate when a student hits you. Protect yourself, stay poised, distance yourself from the student, and call for help immediately.

Words of Grace

*Remember…* The other students in the class are watching how you react and respond to this situation. Your actions and words in this very tough moment can defuse the situation with the aggressive student, model grace and self-control, and help the other students feel safe.

Words of Relationship

*Remember…* When dealing with a student who has hit you, speak calmly with the student and reassure the other students that you're going to take care of the situation.

Words of Respect

*Remember…* Most of your days are spent working hard to understand your middle school or high school students and meet their needs. Unfortunately, this pursuit to understand your students is not always met with

your students seeking to understand you and your needs. Be sure to spend time with your loved ones where your needs are valued and can be met.
Words of Understanding

*Remember…* Your loved ones are there for you when you experience the hardest days of being a teacher. They can offer you encouragement and support when you need it most.
Words of Relationship

*Remember…* Rather than harboring ill feelings for a student who has hit you, demonstrate grace and dig deep to get to the root of the problem and try to understand what triggered this student's anger and aggression.
Words of Grace

*Remember…* Rather than keeping your emotions about the incident to yourself, consider talking with a guidance counselor or an administrator at your school to discuss how you're feeling about the incident and how you're processing it.
Words of Hope

### GTL to Share with the Aggressive Student and the Other Students in the Class, in the Moment:

"Jamie, your behavior just now was against our school policy. I'm going to call the principal and school resource officer immediately."
Words of Accountability

"We are going to discuss this behavior with the principal and your parents."
Words of Accountability

(To the whole class) "Thank you for staying calm and for helping me with this situation. Please stay in your seats and work quietly while I call the principal and the school resource officer."

Words of Guidance

(To the whole class when you are about to go to the principal's office) "Mrs. Jones (another teacher or assistant principal) is going to come and supervise the class while we go to the principal's office."

Words of Unity

### GTL to Share with the Aggressive Student in the Principal's Office:

"You know that I'll work with you to help you in any way I can but hitting me was wrong. It hurt me. We can't hurt each other."

Words of Accountability

"Because of your behavior, you're going to be (state your school's policy for hitting a teacher)". (If your school's policy is an out-of-school suspension, you can say…) "We're going to send home your schoolwork and you'll keep up with your assignments. We're going to call your parents right now and let you explain to them what happened and what you did."

Words of Accountability

(After the phone call with parents) "I appreciate you being honest with your parents about what happened—that's the first step in getting to the truth of what caused you to act that way. Once we know what caused it, we can learn how to prevent it from happening again."

Words of Encouragement

(If the student apologizes to you) "I appreciate your apology, and I accept it and forgive you. I'll make sure you have the schoolwork you need to keep up with your assignments. I'm looking forward to you getting back to class."

Words of Grace

(If the student doesn't apologize to you) "I can see that you're still frustrated and need more time to cool down. I hope with more time, you'll come back to me to apologize. I'll make sure you have the schoolwork you need to keep up with your assignments. I'm looking forward to you getting back to class."

Words of Grace

**GTL to Use When Talking and Communicating with Parents:**

**Phone call from the teacher to the parent to let the student explain what happened in class today when he hit the teacher.**

(This phone call is coming from the principal's office. The principal and the teacher agree that the teacher will lead the phone conversation.)

"Hello! My name is…. I'm Jamie's teacher. Is now a good time for us to talk?"

Words of Respect

"I have Jamie here in the principal's office with me. He's going to tell you what happened."

Words of Accountability

(Jamie tells his parents what happened and is truthful.)

"Because of Jamie's behavior, he's going to be (state your school's policy for hitting a teacher)". (If your school's policy is an out-of-school suspension, you can say…) "An out-of-school suspension doesn't mean he'll get behind in his schoolwork. We're going to send home his schoolwork, and he'll be able to keep up with his assignments."

Words of Accountability

"This just happened a few minutes ago, so Jamie and I really haven't had a chance to talk about what caused this to happen, yet. If he shares more with you while he's home, please let me know. I really want to understand what caused this and how to keep it from happening again."

Words of Unity

"It's important for us to maintain a strong relationship and open communication between home and school."

Words of Relationship

"Before we finish our conversation, I wanted to share that I have enjoyed having Jamie in my class. He is… (share something personal, positive, and specific that you've experienced with Jamie and link it to a positive quality that could help Jamie in his future in high school, college and/or career, and life)."

Words of Encouragement

"Please let me know if you have any questions at all. My hope is for all our students to feel safe, enjoy school, learn as much as they can every day, and be ready for high school and life (use this with middle school students) or college and/or career and life (use this with high school students)."

Words of Hope

## GTL Classroom Activities to Transform Middle School and High School Student Behavior and Your Classroom Culture

### GTL Classroom Activities to Address Middle School and High School Student Conflict in the Classroom

We see these activities as either "in the moment" or a time to pull your students together for classroom conversations to encourage student voice and student engagement in your classroom.

We see the teacher as a facilitator and co-learner during these GTL activities and students as active participants in learning how to "see the classroom through the lens of the teacher" and how to manage their own current behavior for success and their future behavior as they get ready for high school, college and/or a career.

1. (Role-Play GTL Scenario for Students to Practice How to Avoid Conflicts Before They Happen) Before the role-play, take a few minutes to openly discuss some reasons for conflict between students (anger, bullying, embarrassment, feeling insulted, fighting for possessions, greed, jealousy, selfishness, etc.). Select one student to role-play a teacher, and two students to role-play students who are in a conflict. The conflict could be they are angry with each other because one student insulted the other student. Or you could use a different conflict to describe your specific class situation. Allow time for the two students who are in conflict to interact and argue with each other. Then, allow time for the role-playing teacher to respond to the arguing students and give them strategies for avoiding the conflict. Encourage the other students in the class to help the role-playing teacher with what to say and to offer helpful strategies to avoid the conflict. Conclude the role-playing activity with a discussion of how you, as the teacher, would address the students to help avoid the conflict.
2. (Hit the Pause Button for Discussion on Student Behavior Expectations Related to Your School's Policies on Bullying, Cyberbullying, and Fighting and What to Do if You are Bullied and How to Prevent a Fight) Share with the students that you are going to "Hit the Pause Button" on the lesson and take important time to discuss (1) the school policies related to bullying, cyberbullying, and fighting; (2) what to do if you are bullied by someone; and (3) how to prevent a fight. Share with your students your school's policies for bullying, cyberbullying, and fighting. Explain to students how these policies are intended to keep everyone safe at school and to deter these behaviors from happening. Allow time for students to discuss what you

can do if you are being bullied. List those strategies on the board (e.g., 1. Respectfully ask the other student to stop; 2. Walk away and stay away from the other student; 3. Don't bully them back; 4. Find an adult nearby; 5. Talk with your teacher; 6. Ask to talk with the guidance counselor). Discuss how these bully prevention strategies are also very helpful strategies to use to prevent a fight. Conclude the discussion with reminders of how bullying, cyberbullying, and fighting are not acceptable in our class or school, ever.

3. (Getting Ready for Life Discussion about Not Letting Mistakes Define Us and Making Great Choices Now and in Their Future) Share with the students that you're about to have a Getting Ready for Life discussion related to making great choices now and in their future and not letting our mistakes define who we are. Explain to the students how they will face many difficult choices this year and in high school or college/career and in their life. Discuss how each choice you make creates either a positive or a negative chain of events. Then, break the class into small discussion groups. First, ask students to share some of the difficult choices they will be facing this year and in the future. Circulate around the room to listen in on the small group discussions. Then, ask the students to share their personal stories of a series of difficult choices they have made that led to a negative chain of events for them. Also, allow time for the students to share their personal success stories for making a series of great choices that led to a positive chain of events for them. Bring the whole class back together and ask if any group wants to share with the whole class. Remind students how their personal success stories might help and encourage another student to make great choices that result in a positive chain of events for them and their future. Conclude by discussing how it's important for all of us to learn from our mistakes, not allow our mistakes to define us or our future, and share how making great choices will set them up for success for high school, college and/or career, and life.

# 11

# Transforming Your Middle School and High School Classroom Culture into a Great Classroom Culture to Promote High School Readiness, College and/or Career Readiness, and Life Skills

Throughout this book, you've read hundreds of Great Teacher Language (GTL) examples to use with middle school and high school students and parents. Our hope is that you will adopt and integrate these GTL examples and make them your own. Your daily use of GTL with middle school and high school students and parents can transform your classroom culture into a Great Classroom Culture (GCC). A GCC is a culture built on the 11 GTL Word Categories. It's a culture of accountability, encouragement, grace, guidance, high expectations, hope, love, relationships, respect, understanding, and unity. It's a strong and caring culture that will enhance learning! It's a culture that will transform student behavior and parent relationships! The GCC Framework for High School Readiness, College and/or Career Readiness, and Life Skills (see Table 11.1) describes the transformational

**TABLE 11.1** The Great Classroom Culture Framework for High School Readiness, College and/or Career Readiness, and Life Skills

| A Great Classroom Culture Promotes | So That Middle School Students | And High School Students | And Parents |
| --- | --- | --- | --- |
| Accountability | Reach personal accountability in middle school and high school and in their future | Reach personal accountability in high school, college and/or career, and life | Become well-informed supporters of their child and the teacher. |
| Encouragement | Live a better way and become all they can be in middle school and high school and in their future | Live a better way and become all they can be in high school, college and/or career, and life | Feel encouraged about their child and their child's school experiences now and in their future. |
| Grace | Experience and practice the power of forgiveness and second chances in middle school and high school and in their future | Experience and practice the power of forgiveness and second chances in high school, college and/or career, and life | See and hear the power of forgiveness and second chances for their child. |
| Guidance | Practice self-management in middle school and high school and in their future | Practice self-management in high school, college and/or career, and life | Are confident their child is supported and will receive the personalized guidance and assistance they need throughout the year and for their child's future success. |
| High Expectations | Achieve their full potential in middle school and high school and in their future | Achieve their full potential in high school, college and/or career, and life | Will expect their child to achieve their full potential both in school and at home and in their future. |

| | | | |
|---|---|---|---|
| Hope | Hope for and work for a better tomorrow in middle school and high school and in their future | Hope for and work for a better tomorrow in high school, college and/or career, and life | Experience ongoing hope for their child throughout the school year and for their future. |
| Love | Experience and practice the selfless power and purpose of putting others first in middle school and high school and in their future | Experience and practice the selfless power and purpose of putting others first in high school, college and/or career, and life | Know without a doubt their child will experience unconditional care and receive loving accountability throughout the year. |
| Relationships | Develop positive lifelong relationships with others in middle school and high school and in their future | Develop positive lifelong relationships with others in high school, college and/or career, and life | Experience the power of a positive and transformational relationship with you and the school. |
| Respect | Model respect for self and others in middle school and high school and in their future | Model respect for self and others in high school, college and/or career, and life | Feel respected and valued by you. |
| Understanding | Experience and practice empathy for others in middle school and high school and in their future | Experience and practice empathy for others in high school, college and/or career, and life | Are heard, understood, and valued as vital partners in ensuring their child's success now and in their future. |
| Unity | Practice transformational teamwork through collaboration, agreement, and cooperation in middle school and high school and in their future | Practice transformational teamwork through collaboration, agreement, and cooperation in high school, college and/or career, and life | Become personally engaged members of your school community. |

outcomes that middle school and high school students and parents can experience when a teacher promotes the 11 GTL Word Categories in their classroom!

This GCC starts with a teacher who uses GTL and models it for students. The students are impacted by GTL, and their behaviors are transformed. Parents are impacted by GTL, and they can experience the power of a positive and transformational relationship with you and the school.

A GCC is a culture where teachers graciously offer encouragement, grace, guidance, high expectations, hope, love, and understanding to every middle school and high school student and to all parents. It's a culture where teachers work to develop relationships, share mutual respect, and promote unity with all students and their parents. It's a culture where teachers hold themselves and their students accountable to positive behavior expectations and are willing to share those behavior expectations with parents and ask for their support.

A GCC reflects a commitment to all the characteristics of the 11 GTL Word Categories. When middle school and high school teachers use GTL and promote the 11 GTL Word Categories to build a GCC, the results are transformational! For example, in a GCC, when middle school and high school teachers use *Words of Encouragement* and promote *Encouragement*, students are encouraged to be all they can be, and they begin to encourage other students. *Encouragement* increases. When students hear *Words of Grace* and experience *Grace* from their teacher, they experience the power of forgiveness and second chances, and they begin to show grace to other students. *Grace* increases. When teachers build *Relationships* with students, students begin to build *Relationships* with one another. *Relationships* increase. When teachers provide students with *Respectful Guidance* toward great behavior choices, students learn how to become self-managed in middle school and high school and in their future. The next section will describe the 11 GTL Characteristics of a GCC and the great transformations that can happen for middle school and high school students.

## The 11 GTL Characteristics of a Great Classroom Culture

A GCC promotes *Accountability*. In a classroom culture that promotes *Accountability*, teachers and students are held *Accountable* for their words and actions. In middle school and high school classrooms, teacher behavior expectations, student behavior expectations, group work norms, and classroom rules are jointly determined on the first day of school and in the days that follow. School policies are shared and discussed together as well. To promote *Unity*, parents are included in the process by being asked to sign the Student/Teacher/Parent Agreement describing these behavior expectations, classroom rules, group work norms, and school policies. As these behavior expectations, group work norms, classroom rules, and school policies are discussed frequently, students are *Encouraged* to make great behavior choices, which empowers them to practice personal *Accountability*. Personal *Accountability* is a crucial life skill for middle school students in the present and as they enter the world of high school. The same is true for high school students now and as they enter college or begin a chosen career or start a family. As teachers use Words of *Accountability* and promote a *Culture of Accountability* in their classrooms, they provide a path for middle school and high school students to develop personal *Accountability* now and in their future.

A GCC promotes *Encouragement*. In a classroom culture that promotes *Encouragement*, teachers *Encourage* themselves (GTL Reminders to Self) and their middle school and high school students (GTL to Share with Students) to be the best they can be both academically and in their personal lives. Students are *Encouraged* and *Guided* to reach their potential in middle school, in high school, and in their future. Teachers *Encourage* themselves and their students with the confidence to do the right thing for themselves and to overcome their fears and keep on trying. When teachers *Encourage* parents about their child and their child's school experiences, they positively inspire parents and build powerful *Relationships* with them. As middle school students experience the power of a *Culture of Encouragement*, they begin to have the courage to overcome the challenges, obstacles, barriers, failures, defeats, fears, and apathy in middle school and develop the courage to move into high school ready to face and overcome those same issues. Experiencing the power of a *Culture of Encouragement* offers high school students the same courage to overcome the challenges, obstacles, barriers, failures, defeats, fears, and apathy of high school and develop the courage to move forward into college and/or a career and into their adult life ready to face and overcome those same realities.

A GCC promotes *Grace*. In a classroom culture that promotes *Grace*, teachers demonstrate *Understanding, Love*, patience, and *Respect* for all middle school and high school students despite what they choose to do, hold them *Accountable* for those choices, and then offer them *Grace* to get it right the next time. Teachers share unconditional *Love* and support for students despite what those students may choose to do. In a *Culture of Grace*, teachers do not harbor ill feelings toward students; instead, teachers practice the act of forgiveness and *Guide* their students to practice the act of forgiveness toward others as well. *Grace* is demonstrated to parents when teachers offer their child another chance to get it right and forgive their child's past mistakes. When teachers promote a *Culture of Grace*, middle school students experience the power of forgiveness and realize the reality of second chances. High school presents an excellent opportunity for middle school students to begin anew and experience the *Hope* that *Grace* offers them. Students in high school learn that when *Grace* is offered to them, they are given a second chance to get it right, which can impact their future plans for college and/or a career and life.

A GCC promotes *Guidance*. In a classroom culture that promotes *Guidance*, teachers are the *Guide* for their middle school and high school students both academically and behaviorally. As teachers *Guide* their students, they give them a positive and supportive path to great behavior choices. Teachers offer their students advice to *Guide* them all along the way. They offer students specific advice—*Next time try this or do this*—*Consider doing this*—*Here's another way*. As teachers *Respectfully Guide* their students, they offer them an opportunity to improve both academically and behaviorally. Teachers demonstrate *Guidance* when they inform parents of the assistance they and the school will provide to their child. The end goal of a culture of *Guidance* is when students choose to be self-managed in their behavior choices and their learning. When middle school students experience a *Culture of Guidance*, they learn how to manage their behavior choices in both middle school and high school. This self-management skill *Guides* students into making great behavior choices. When these same students enter high school and move into college and/or a career, they use those self-management skills to enable them to continue making their own great behavior choices.

A GCC promotes *High Expectations*. In a classroom culture that promotes *High Expectations*, teachers set the bar high by expecting the best from all middle school and high school students and themselves. When teachers set *High Expectations* with *Guidance* for their students, they help their students to envision and pursue their best in middle school and high school and when planning their future. Setting *High Expectations* and conveying the anticipation that all students will meet them creates a *Culture of High Expectations* that expects all middle school and high school students to achieve their full potential both academically and behaviorally in school and in their future. Sharing *High Expectations* with parents demonstrates how teachers will help their child envision and pursue their best schoolwork and behavior in the present, which will help them achieve higher levels of success in their future.

A GCC promotes *Hope*. In a classroom culture that promotes *Hope*, middle school and high school students and teachers are *Encouraged* to see themselves and others with great potential. Teachers and students dare to dream: dream of how they can actually achieve more than they expected. Middle school and high school students gain the confidence that what they *Hope* for—what they dream of—can happen! *Hope* can spark students' interests and inspire them to learn more than ever before and change their behavior and life choices. When teachers share *Hope* with parents, they inspire parents to look beyond the current circumstances and expect greater things for their child. When middle school students experience a *Culture of Hope*, they dare to dream of what they can achieve in high school and in their future as well as gain the confidence to do so. The same is true for high school students who experience a *Culture of Hope*. Their dreams of what they can achieve and the confidence to achieve more than they expected exist in the present and move into college and/or a career and into their future life as an adult.

A GCC promotes *Love*. This *Love* is never to be confused with a romantic love nor should it be shared without *Accountability*. In a classroom culture that promotes *Love*, teachers demonstrate an unconditional *Love* and care for middle school and high school students. Students feel valued and supported while being held *Accountable* for the choices they make. In a *Culture of Love*, teachers demonstrate the patience to endure students' misbehavior choices, dig deep to *Understand* each student's needs, and make an unwavering commitment to the belief that all students can improve. As teachers demonstrate *Love* and care for middle school and high school students, they inspire their students to use their own words and actions to help other students and practice empathy for themselves and others. When teachers demonstrate *Love* and care for parents and their child, they touch parents' hearts and trusting *Relationships* begin to develop. As middle school students get ready for high school and their future and high school students get ready for college and/or a career, experiencing a *Culture of Love* gives them the support and feelings of value they need to care for themselves and others.

A GCC promotes building *Relationships*. In a classroom culture that promotes building *Relationships* with all students, teachers are committed to getting to know every one of their middle school and high school students personally. Teachers make a conscious effort to create meaningful connections with students by showing each student they are valued and worth their time and attention. Middle school and high school students trust their teacher when they feel emotionally safe and know that their teacher *Loves* and cares about them and wants the best for them. As teachers build *Relationships* with their students, they talk with students and spend time individually with them to discover their passions, talents, interests, and their dreams for their future. When teachers build *Relationships* with students, they demonstrate a desire to work with students to break down walls, build bridges, and reach common ground. When teachers build *Relationships* with parents, they establish a trusting, caring, *Respectful*, and positive connection with every parent. In middle school and high school classrooms, *Relationships* with other students are crucial. The same is true of life. Relationships are everything! As middle school students move into high school, developing *Relationships* with fellow students is important. High school students who move on to college or a career will benefit tremendously by learning how to build strong *Relationships* with fellow students and/or coworkers and later with their own family members.

A GCC promotes *Respect*. In a classroom culture that promotes *Respect*, teachers demonstrate a careful consideration and appreciation for all middle school and high school students and themselves. When teachers make a deliberate attempt to *Understand* a middle school or a high school student's perspective about their behavior, their learning, or a life situation, they demonstrate *Respect* for students and their needs. As teachers model *Respect* for themselves and their students, it reveals a desire to value all students and demonstrates a proper regard for the dignity of their own character and the character of their students. As teachers promote a *Culture of Respect* with middle school and high school students, it builds a model for mutual *Respect* between the teacher and all students. When teachers use words of *Respect* with parents, it demonstrates an intentional consideration and appreciation for all parents, and parents feel *Respected* and valued. As middle school students prepare for high school and as high school students prepare for college and/or a career, experiencing and understanding respect for others and themselves will enable them to demonstrate that same respect for new teachers, new acquaintances, new coworkers, themselves, and others.

A GCC promotes *Understanding*. In a classroom culture that promotes *Understanding*, teachers demonstrate a conscious and deliberate effort to *Understand* their middle school and high school students' perspective in all situations. When individual student behavior or learning issues arise, teachers intentionally attempt to put themselves in the student's position to see things and *Understand* things from their perspective. Teachers want to

*Understand* what's going on with the student and ask thoughtful questions to get to the root of the problem. As teachers spend quality time with individual middle school and high school students and attempt to *Understand* their perspective, *Relationships* of trust are built. In a *Culture of Understanding*, the ultimate goal is for teachers and students to experience and practice empathy for others. When teachers seek to *Understand* the parents' perspective, parents feel heard, understood, and valued as vital partners in ensuring their child's success. As middle school students navigate middle school and prepare for high school and as high school students navigate high school and prepare for college and/or a career, a *Culture of Understanding* will enable them to practice empathy for other teachers, other students, and future coworkers and family members.

A GCC promotes *Unity*. In a classroom culture that promotes *Unity*, teachers *Encourage* a sense of belonging by ensuring that all middle school and high school students know they are valued and their participation in class activities and school events is vital to the class team and the school team. In a *Culture of Unity*, the goal is to transform a group of individuals into a team culture. Teachers in middle school and high school promote a *Culture of Unity* as they actively *Encourage* school pride along with a sense of belonging to their classroom community and the school community. Promoting a sense of school pride and a team culture encourages collaboration, agreement, and cooperation with your students. Teachers also promote *Unity* with parents by inviting and *Encouraging* them to be active team members of the classroom and the school community. As middle school students prepare for high school and as high school students prepare for college and/or a career, a *Culture of Unity* will enable them to experience pride in working together as a team to support their fellow students, their school, their coworkers, their family members, and their community.

Now that you have read this book, our hope is that you will be encouraged, excited, and ready to try GTL! We've seen amazing transformations happen when teachers use it and share it with middle school and high school students and parents. Student behavior is transformed, parent relationships are transformed, and your classroom culture is transformed. A GCC of collaboration, teamwork, and strong relationships among teachers, students, and their parents emerges when teachers use GTL. Other transformational changes can happen across your school community as you share and discuss GTL with other educators in your school. GTL and a GCC can break the burnout-to-dropout cycle and prevent student burnout, parent burnout, and teacher burnout. Using GTL and creating a GCC promote vitality for you and your school community! The GTL Framework and the GCC Framework for High School Readiness, College and/or Career Readiness, and Life Skills can revitalize and support the existing student behavior management plans in your school. Students, parents, and teachers experience a school culture with vitality where they feel respected, valued, and successful. Students, parents, teachers, and **you** get to experience a renewed school culture in a transformed way—where we all work together to experience happiness, hope, and joy every day!

# Index of GTL Student Behavior Scenarios

Chapter 3: What Do Great Teachers Say on the First Day of School and the Days that Follow?

Standard 3.1: Setting High Expectations for All
Standard 3.2: Establishing the Rules and Behavior Expectations for Success
Standard 3.3: Creating a Culture of Community and Teamwork
Standard 3.4: Encouraging Life-Long Self-Management
Standard 3.5: Leading by Example
Standard 3.6: Building Relationships with Students and Their Families

Chapter 4: What Do Great Teachers Say When a Student Seems Apathetic, Passively Disengaged, and/or Disconnected from School?

Scenario 4.1: A Student is Chronically Absent from School.
Scenario 4.2: A Student is Consistently Tardy to School or to a Particular Class.
Scenario 4.3: A Student is Skipping School All Day or Skipping a Particular Class During the Day.
Scenario 4.4: A Student is Sleeping During Class.
Scenario 4.5: A Student is Not Working on His Assignment and Looks Confused, Stressed, Or Frustrated.
Scenario 4.6: A Student Is Not Paying Attention to the Lesson, Is Uninterested, or Seems to Be Daydreaming In Class.
Scenario 4.7: A Student Never Verbally Participates In Class.
Scenario 4.8: A Passively Disengaged Student Has Failing Grades In Your Class.

Chapter 5: What Do Great Teachers Say to Encourage Proper Use of Technology and Devices in the Classroom

Scenario 5.1: A Student is Off-task and Texting on His/Her Phone.

Scenario 5.2: A Student is Off-task, Playing a Video Game, Watching a Video, or Watching a Movie on His Phone/Computer.

Scenario 5.3: A Student is Off-task and Listening to Music on His/Her Phone (Using Ear Buds).

Scenario 5.4: A Student is Off-task and Searching Online for Personal Reasons.

Scenario 5.5: A Student is Plagiarizing Other People's Work and/Or Copying Answers from Online Sources.

Chapter 6: What Do Great Teachers Say When a Student is an Attention Seeker?

Scenario 6.1: A Student is Intentionally Asking Questions to Distract the Teacher Away From the Lesson.

Scenario 6.2: A Student Is Up Out of His/Her Seat, Looking at Another Student's Phone, Laughing, and Socializing with Other Students.

Scenario 6.3: A Student is Annoying Another Student and Wanting Their Attention Either Verbally, in Writing, Or by Texting.

Scenario 6.4: A Student is Being the Class Entertainer and/or Social Influencer.

Scenario 6.5: A Student is Verbally Monopolizing the Lesson by Answering Every Question or Constantly Asking Questions.

Scenario 6.6: A Student is Constantly Talking with Other Students During the Lesson.

Chapter 7: What Do Great Teachers Say When a Student Outburst Happens?

Scenario 7.1: A Student Yells Out, "This Is So Boring!"

Scenario 7.2: A Student Yells Out, "I'm Lost! I Don't Understand!"

Scenario 7.3: A Student Yells Out, "Why Do We Have to Do This…? When Are We Ever Going to Need This or Use This?"

Scenario 7.4: A Student Yells Out Profanity, "@#$%!"

Scenario 7.5: A Student Yells Out a Verbally Aggressive Outburst and/or Acts Out a Physically Aggressive Outburst.

Chapter 8: What Do Great Teachers Say When a Student Does Not Show Respect for Themselves or Others?

Scenario 8.1: A Student is Calling Other Students Disrespectful Names and/or Making Fun of Other Students.

Scenario 8.2: A Student is Making Inappropriate Gestures Toward Other Students and/or the Teacher.

Scenario 8.3: A Student is Verbally Disrespectful to the Teacher.

Scenario 8.4: A Student is Interrupting Another Student and/or the Teacher.

Scenario 8.5: A Student is Taking Things That Do Not Belong to Him/Her.

Scenario 8.6: A Student is Demonstrating a Lack of Self-Respect.

Chapter 9: What Do Great Teachers Say When a Student Refuses to Cooperate or Challenges Them?

Scenario 9.1: A Student Consistently Asks Questions that Challenge You and/or the Lesson You Are Teaching

Scenario 9.2: A Student Disagrees With You and Says, "You're Wrong! That's Not What We Were Taught Before!"

Scenario 9.3: A Student Refuses to Cooperate with You and Says, "You're Not My Mom! You Can't Tell Me What To Do! You Can't Make Me Do This Work!"

Scenario 9.4: A Student is Outwardly Angry and Blatantly Disrespectful Toward You.

Chapter 10: What Do Great Teachers Say When a Student Conflict Occurs?

Scenario 10.1: Two Students Are in a Small Disagreement and Are Not Getting Along With One Another.

Scenario 10.2: Two Students Are Arguing with One Another.

Scenario 10.3: A Student Pushes and/or Shoves Another Student.
Scenario 10.4: A Student Hits Another Student.
Scenario 10.5: A Student is Bullying Another Student.
Scenario 10.6: A Student is Cyberbullying Another Student.
Scenario 10.7: Two Students Are Physically Fighting.
Scenario 10.8: A Student Hits the Teacher.

For Product Safety Concerns and Information please contact our EU
representative GPSR@taylorandfrancis.com
Taylor & Francis Verlag GmbH, Kaufingerstraße 24, 80331 München, Germany

www.ingramcontent.com/pod-product-compliance
Lightning Source LLC
Chambersburg PA
CBHW050626300426
44112CB00012B/1669